DOVER · THRIFT · EDITIONS

The Merry Wives of Windsor

WILLIAM SHAKESPEARE

DOVER PUBLICATIONS, INC.
Mineola, New York

DOVER THRIFT EDITIONS

GENERAL EDITOR: PAUL NEGRI
EDITOR OF THIS VOLUME: SUSAN L. RATTINER

Copyright

Theatrical Rights

Bibliographical Note

This Dover edition, first published in 2000, contains the unabridged text of *The Merry Wives of Windsor* as published in Volume IV of *The Caxton Edition of the Complete Works of William Shakespeare*, Caxton Publishing Company, London, n.d. The Note was prepared specially for this edition.

Library of Congress Cataloging-in-Publication Data

Shakespeare, William, 1564–1616.
    The merry wives of Windsor / William Shakespeare.
        p. cm. — (Dover thrift editions)
    "Contains the unabridged text of The merry wives of Windsor as published in volume IV of the Caxton edition of The complete works of William Shakespeare, Caxton Publishing Company, London"—T.p. verso.
    ISBN 0-486-41422-1
    1. Falstaff, John, Sir (Fictitious character)—Drama. 2. Married women—Drama. 3. Windsor (Berkshire, England)—Drama. I. Title. II. Series.

PR2826 .A1 2000
822.3'3—dc21

00-031779

Manufactured in the United States of America
Dover Publications, Inc., 31 East 2nd Street, Mineola, N.Y. 11501

Note

The Merry Wives of Windsor is an unusual example of William Shakespeare's (1564–1616) comedic talent. Virtually his only play that portrays middle-class country life in any way, it also is the only one set in Windsor, where it was probably first performed. The setting of the farce is at once understandable since it was supposedly written at the express request of Queen Elizabeth I after she had seen the performances of both parts of *Henry IV*. The queen had grown so enamored of Falstaff that she commanded Shakespeare to write a play detailing the character's exploits in love. Not only did the skillful dramatist comply with her order, but he is also said to have completed it in a fortnight. The first recorded mention of this can be found in John Dennis's preface to the 1702 adaptation of the play.

One of his great comedies, *The Merry Wives of Windsor* might have been written as early as 1597, as its first performance is thought to have occurred during the Feast of St. George, which was the initiation ceremony for the newly elected Knights of the Garter. An early version of the play, entered into the Stationers' Register in January 1602, was later discovered to be a "bad quarto," a mangled form of the play reconstructed from memory by one of the actors. The authoritative text of the play was first published in 1623 in the First Folio, a collected edition of Shakespeare's plays.

Unlike many of Shakespeare's works, *The Merry Wives of Windsor* owes little of its plot to previous writers. If conjecture can be believed—that Shakespeare wrote and performed the play all within fourteen days—then one can only assume that the dramatist must have revived events and characters from previous plays, perhaps ones already owned by his theatre company. Although no specific source is known, some critics infer that the comic devices in the play correspond with Italian popular comedy of the time, specifically Straparola's *Le Tredici Piacevoli Notte*, which was then available in English translations.

Contents

Dramatis Personæ[1]

SIR JOHN FALSTAFF.

FENTON, a gentleman.

SHALLOW, a country justice.

SLENDER, cousin to Shallow.

FORD,
PAGE, } two gentlemen dwelling at Windsor.

WILLIAM PAGE, a boy, son to Page.

SIR HUGH EVANS, a Welsh parson.

DOCTOR CAIUS, a French physician.

HOST of the Garter Inn.

BARDOLPH,
PISTOL, } sharpers attending on Falstaff.
NYM,

ROBIN, page to Falstaff.

SIMPLE, servant to Slender.

RUGBY, servant to Doctor Caius.

MISTRESS FORD.

MISTRESS PAGE.

ANNE PAGE, her daughter.

MISTRESS QUICKLY, servant to Doctor Caius.

Servants to Page, Ford, etc.

SCENE — *Windsor, and the neighbourhood*

[1]An imperfect sketch of this play was first published in quarto in 1602, and was reissued in 1619. A complete version first appeared in the First Folio of 1623, and this was reissued in a Third Quarto in 1630. The Folio first divided the text into acts and scenes. But there is no list of "dramatis personæ." This was first supplied by Nicholas Rowe in his edition of Shakespeare's works, 1709.

ACT I.

Scene I. *Windsor. Before Page's House.*

Enter Justice Shallow, Slender, *and* Sir Hugh Evans

Shallow. Sir Hugh, persuade me not; I will make a Star-chamber matter[1] of it: if he were twenty Sir John Falstaffs, he shall not abuse Robert Shallow, esquire.

Slen. In the county of Gloucester, justice of peace and "Coram."[2]

Shal. Ay, cousin Slender, and "Custalorum."

Slen. Ay, and "Rato-lorum" too; and a gentleman born, master parson; who writes himself "Armigero, in any bill, warrant, quittance, or obligation, "Armigero."

Shal. Ay, that I do; and have done any time these three hundred years.

Slen. All his successors gone before him hath done 't; and all his ancestors that come after him may: they may give the dozen white luces[3] in their coat.

Shal. It is an old coat.

Evans. The dozen white louses[4] do become an old coat well; it agrees well, passant; it is a familiar beast to man, and signifies love.

---

[1]*Star-chamber matter*] Matter for the Court of Star Chamber, which had cognizance of all riots.

[2]*"Coram"*] Slender here and in his next speech is confusedly recalling the official Latin titles of a justice of the peace. The word "quorum," which he mispronounces "coram," was prominent in the formal commission, which also designated a justice "custos rotulorum." Justice Shallow would sign his attestations "*Coram* me Roberto Shallow, *armigero*" (*i.e.* arms-bearer, esquire).

[3]*dozen white luces*] "Luce" was the name commonly applied to a full-grown and ageing pike. Shallow is a caricature sketch of Sir Thomas *Lucy* of Charlecote, who is reputed to have punished Shakespeare in his youth for poaching in his park. Sir Thomas bore on his heraldic shield three *luces* hauriant argent.

[4]*louses*] Sir Hugh's punning confusion of "luce" with "louse" ("a familiar beast to man") implies that he pronounced the two words alike.

1

SHAL.   The luce is the fresh fish; the salt fish is an old coat.[5]

SLEN.   I may quarter,[6] coz.

SHAL.   You may, by marrying.

EVANS.   It is marring indeed, if he quarter it.

SHAL.   Not a whit.

EVANS.   Yes, py'r lady; if he has a quarter of your coat, there is but three skirts for yourself, in my simple conjectures: but that is all one. If Sir John Falstaff have committed disparagements unto you, I am of the church, and will be glad to do my benevolence to make atonements and comprimises between you.

SHAL.   The council[7] shall hear it; it is a riot.

EVANS.   It is not meet the council hear a riot; there is no fear of Got in a riot: the council, look you, shall desire to hear the fear of Got, and not to hear a riot; take your vizaments in that.[8]

SHAL.   Ha! o' my life, if I were young again, the sword should end it.

EVANS.   It is petter that friends is the sword, and end it: and there is also another device in my prain, which peradventure prings goot discretions with it:—there is Anne Page, which is daughter to Master Thomas Page,[9] which is pretty virginity.

SLEN.   Mistress Anne Page? She has brown hair, and speaks small[10] like a woman.

EVANS.   It is that fery person for all the orld, as just as you will desire; and seven hundred pounds of moneys, and gold and silver, is her grandsire upon his death's-bed (Got deliver to a joyful resurrections!) give, when she is able to overtake seventeen years old: it were a goot motion if we leave our pribbles and prabbles,[11] and desire a marriage between Master Abraham and Mistress Anne Page.

SLEN.   Did her grandsire leave her seven hundred pound?

EVANS.   Ay, and her father is make her a petter penny.

---

[5]These lines are difficult to explain. Shallow, by way of denying Evans's suggestion of agreement between "luces" and "an old coat," points out that the pike, which lives in *fresh* water, can have no staleness about it; such an attribute is only possible in *salted* fish (of the sea), which can therefore be alone identified with an old cast-off coat.

[6]*quarter*] a technical term in heraldry; used as a verb, it means to fill a compartment of a shield with armorial bearings other than those of one's father—*e.g.* those of one's wife.

[7]*council*] the star-chamber, which was a committee of the privy council.

[8]*take . . . that*] be sure of that. "Vizaments" is a blunder for "advisements" counsels, deliberations.

[9]*Thomas Page*] This is the original reading. Elsewhere, II, i, and V, v, Page is called "George." "Thomas" is probably an oversight of the author.

[10]*speaks small*] speaks in a low voice.

[11]*pribbles and prabbles*] The Welshman's mispronunciation of bribble-brabble, a common reduplicated form of "brabble," discordant babble, vain chatter.

SLEN.   I know the young gentlewoman; she has good gifts.

EVANS.   Seven hundred pounds and possibilities is goot gifts.

SHAL.   Well, let us see honest Master Page. Is Falstaff there?

EVANS.   Shall I tell you a lie? I do despise a liar as I do despise one that is false, or as I despise one that is not true. The knight, Sir John, is there; and, I beseech you, be ruled by your well-willers. I will peat the door for Master Page. [*Knocks*] What, hoa! Got pless your house here!

PAGE. [*within*]   Who's there?

Enter PAGE

EVANS.   Here is Got's plessing, and your friend, and Justice Shallow; and here young Master Slender, that peradventures shall tell you another tale, if matters grow to your likings.

PAGE.   I am glad to see your worships well. I thank you for my venison, Master Shallow.

SHAL.   Master Page, I am glad to see you: much good do it your good heart! I wished your venison better; it was ill killed. How doth good Mistress Page?—and I thank you always with my heart, la! with my heart.

PAGE.   Sir, I thank you.

SHAL.   Sir, I thank you; by yea and no, I do.

PAGE.   I am glad to see you, good Master Slender.

SLEN.   How does your fallow greyhound, sir? I heard say he was outrun on Cotsall.[12]

PAGE.   It could not be judged, sir.

SLEN.   You'll not confess, you'll not confess.

SHAL.   That he will not. 'T is your fault; 't is your fault; 't is a good dog.

PAGE.   A cur, sir.

SHAL.   Sir, he's a good dog, and a fair dog: can there be more said? he is good and fair. Is Sir John Falstaff here?

PAGE.   Sir, he is within; and I would I could do a good office between you.

EVANS.   It is spoke as a Christians ought to speak.

SHAL.   He hath wronged me, Master Page.

PAGE.   Sir, he doth in some sort confess it.

SHAL.   If it be confessed, it is not redressed: is not that so, Master Page? He hath wronged me; indeed he hath; at a word, he hath, believe me: Robert Shallow, esquire, saith, he is wronged.

PAGE.   Here comes Sir John.

---

[12]*Cotsall*] The local pronunciation of Cotswold. On the Cotswold hills, in Gloucestershire, coursing matches and meetings for rural sports were frequently held.

Enter SIR JOHN FALSTAFF, BARDOLPH, NYM, *and* PISTOL

FAL.   Now, Master Shallow, you'll complain of me to the king?

SHAL.   Knight, you have beaten my men, killed my deer, and broke open my lodge.

FAL.   But not kissed your keeper's daughter?

SHAL.   Tut, a pin! this shall be answered.

FAL.   I will answer it straight; I have done all this. That is now answered.

SHAL.   The council shall know this.

FAL.   'T were better for you if it were known in counsel:[13] you'll be laughed at.

EVANS.   Pauca verba, Sir John; Goot worts.[14]

FAL.   Goot worts! good cabbage. Slender, I broke your head: what matter have you against me?

SLEN.   Marry, sir, I have matter in my head against you; and against your cony-catching rascals, Bardolph, Nym, and Pistol.

BARD.   You Banbury cheese![15]

SLEN.   Ay, it is no matter.

PIST.   How now, Mephostophilus![16]

SLEN.   Ay, it is no matter.

NYM.   Slice, I say! pauca, pauca: slice![17] that's my humour.

SLEN.   Where's Simple, my man? Can you tell, cousin?

EVANS.   Peace, I pray you. Now let us understand. There is three umpires in this matter, as I understand; that is, Master Page, fidelicet Master Page; and there is myself, fidelicet myself; and the three party is, lastly and finally, mine host of the Garter.

PAGE.   We three, to hear it and end it between them.

EVANS.   Fery goot: I will make a prief of it in my note-book; and we will afterwards ork upon the cause with as great discreetly as we can.

FAL.   Pistol!

PIST.   He hears with ears.

EVANS.   The tevil and his tam! what phrase is this, "He hears with ear"? why, it is affectations.

FAL.   Pistol, did you pick Master Slender's purse?

SLEN.   Ay, by these gloves, did he, or I would I might never come in

---

[13]*known in counsel*] kept secret.

[14]*worts*] vegetables, of which the "cole-wort" or cabbage is one of the commonest species.

[15]*Banbury cheese*] flat, thin cheese.

[16]*Mephostophilus*] A probable reference to Marlowe's tragedy of *Dr. Faustus.*

[17]*Slice . . . pauca*] Nym echoes Evans' exclamation "pauca verba." "Slice" is a characteristic allusion to the sword.

mine own great chamber again else, of seven groats in mill-
sixpences, and two Edward shovel-boards, that cost me two
shilling and two pence a-piece[18] of Yead[19] Miller, by these gloves.

FAL.   Is this true, Pistol?

EVANS.   No; it is false, if it is a pick-purse.

PIST.   Ha, thou mountain-foreigner! Sir John and master mine,
    I combat challenge of this latten bilbo.[20]
    Word of denial in thy labras[21] here!
    Word of denial: froth and scum, thou liest!

SLEN.   By these gloves, then, 't was he.

NYM.   Be advised, sir, and pass good humours: I will say "marry trap"[22]
    with you, if you run the nuthook's humour on me; that is the very
    note of it.

SLEN.   By this hat, then, he in the red face had it; for though I cannot
    remember what I did when you made me drunk, yet I am not al-
    together an ass.

FAL.   What say you, Scarlet and John?[23]

BARD.   Why, sir, for my part, I say the gentleman had drunk himself
    out of his five sentences.

EVANS.   It is his five senses: fie, what the ignorance is!

BARD.   And being fap,[24] sir, was, as they say, cashiered; and so con-
    clusions passed the careires.[25]

SLEN.   Ay, you spake in Latin then too; but 't is no matter: I'll ne'er be
    drunk whilst I live again, but in honest, civil, godly company, for
    this trick: if I be drunk, I'll be drunk with those that have the fear
    of God, and not with drunken knaves.

EVANS.   So Got udge me, that is a virtuous mind.

FAL.   You hear all these matters denied, gentlemen; you hear it.

---

[18]*seven groats . . . a-piece*] groats, *i.e.* four-penny pieces, were coins of very old standing;
milled or stamped sixpences were first coined in 1561. "Edward shovel-boards" were
broad and heavy shilling-pieces of Edward VI's reign, and came to be used as coun-
ters or discs in the popular game of shovel-board, which in principle resembles the
more modern game of "squayles." Slender's words indicate that the value of Edward
VI's shillings had greatly appreciated; but his figures are not to be depended on. Seven
groats (of four-pence each) could not be converted into sixpence's.

[19]*Yead*] A colloquial form of Ned.

[20]*latten bilbo*] Slender is compared to a sword blade.

[21]*labras*] Pistol bombastically uses the Spanish word for lips.

[22]*I will say "marry trap"*] I will catch you (cry quits with you), if you play the "nuthook"
(*i.e.* constable or catchpole) with me.

[23]*Scarlet and John*] The names of two followers of Robin Hood. "Scarlet" alludes to
Bardolph's red face.

[24]*fap*] drunken; probably from "vappa," a drunken person.

[25]*passed the careires*] galloped on at full speed; a technical term of the equestrian
menage, or art of riding.

Enter ANNE PAGE, *with wine;* MISTRESS FORD *and* MISTRESS PAGE,
  following

PAGE.   Nay, daughter, carry the wine in; we'll drink within.
                                              [*Exit* ANNE PAGE.
SLEN.   O heaven! this is Mistress Anne Page.
PAGE.   How now, Mistress Ford!
FAL.   Mistress Ford, by my troth, you are very well met: by your leave,
    good mistress.   [*Kisses her.*
PAGE.   Wife, bid these gentlemen welcome. Come, we have a hot
    venison pasty to dinner: come, gentlemen, I hope we shall drink
    down all unkindness.
                            [*Exeunt all except* SHAL., SLEN., *and* EVANS.
SLEN.   I had rather than forty shillings I had my Book of Songs and
    Sonnets[26] here.

Enter SIMPLE

    How now, Simple! where have you been? I must wait on myself,
    must I? You have not the Book of Riddles[27] about you, have you?
SIM.   Book of Riddles! why, did you not lend it to Alice Shortcake
    upon All-hallowmas last, a fortnight afore Michaelmas?[28]
SHAL.   Come, coz; come, coz; we stay for you. A word with you, coz;
    marry, this, coz: there is, as 't were, a tender, a kind of tender,
    made afar off by Sir Hugh here. Do you understand me?
SLEN.   Ay, sir, you shall find me reasonable; if it be so, I shall do that
    that is reason.
SHAL.   Nay, but understand me.
SLEN.   So I do, sir.
EVANS.   Give ear to his motions, Master Slender: I will description the
    matter to you, if you be capacity of it.
SLEN.   Nay, I will do as my cousin Shallow says: I pray you, pardon
    me; he's a justice of peace in his country, simple though I stand
    here.
EVANS.   But that is not the question: the question is concerning your
    marriage.

[26]*Book of Songs and Sonnets*] Slender seeks amatory verse wherewith to court Anne
    Page. The book he specifies is probably the popular poetic miscellany, generally
    called *Tottel's Miscellany,* but really entitled *Songes and Sonnetes,* 1557. An eighth
    edition appeared in 1587.
[27]*Book of Riddles*] *The Booke of Mery Riddles* was very popular in the 16th and 17th cen-
    turies, though no edition earlier than that of 1600 seems to be extant.
[28]*All-hallowmas last . . . Michaelmas*] Slender seems to confuse Michaelmas (29
    September) with Martlemas or Martinmas (11 November). All-hallowmas (All Saints,
    1 November) comes some five weeks after Michaelmas, but ten days "afore"
    Martlemas.

SHAL. Ay, there's the point, sir.

EVANS. Marry, is it; the very point of it; to Mistress Anne Page.

SLEN. Why, if it be so, I will marry her upon any reasonable demands.

EVANS. But can you affection the 'oman? Let us command to know that of your mouth or of your lips; for divers philosophers hold that the lips is parcel of the mouth. Therefore, precisely, can you carry your good will to the maid?

SHAL. Cousin Abraham Slender, can you love her?

SLEN. I hope, sir, I will do as it shall become one that would do reason.

EVANS. Nay, Got's lords and his ladies! you must speak possitable, if you can carry her your desires towards her.

SHAL. That you must. Will you, upon good dowry, marry her?

SLEN. I will do a greater thing than that, upon your request, cousin, in any reason.

SHAL. Nay, conceive me, conceive me, sweet coz: what I do is to pleasure you, coz. Can you love the maid?

SLEN. I will marry her, sir, at your request: but if there be no great love in the beginning, yet heaven may decrease it upon better acquaintance, when we are married and have more occasion to know one another; I hope, upon familiarity will grow more contempt: but if you say, "Marry her," I will marry her; that I am freely dissolved, and dissolutely.

EVANS. It is a fery discretion answer; save the fall is in the ort[29] "dissolutely:" the ort is, according to our meaning, "resolutely:" his meaning is good.

SHAL. Ay, I think my cousin meant well.

SLEN. Ay, or else I would I might be hanged, la!

SHAL. Here comes fair Mistress Anne.

Re-enter ANNE PAGE

Would I were young for your sake, Mistress Anne!

ANNE. The dinner is on the table; my father desires your worships' company.

SHAL. I will wait on him, fair Mistress Anne.

EVANS. Od's plessed will! I will not be absence at the grace.

[*Exeunt* SHALLOW *and* EVANS.

ANNE. Will 't please your worship to come in, sir?

SLEN. No, I thank you, forsooth, heartily; I am very well.

---

[29]*fall . . . ort*] Fall is a mispronunciation of "fault," as "ort" is of "word."

ANNE.   The dinner attends you, sir.

SLEN.   I am not a-hungry, I thank you, forsooth. Go, sirrah, for all you
are my man, go wait upon my cousin Shallow. [*Exit* SIMPLE.] A
justice of peace sometime may be beholding to his friend for a
man. I keep but three men and a boy yet, till my mother be dead:
but what though? yet I live like a poor gentleman born.

ANNE.   I may not go in without your worship: they will not sit till you
come.

SLEN.   I' faith, I'll eat nothing; I thank you as much as though I did.

ANNE.   I pray you, sir, walk in.

SLEN.   I had rather walk here, I thank you. I bruised my shin th' other
day with playing at sword and dagger with a master of fence; three
veneys for a dish of stewed prunes;[30] and, by my troth, I cannot
abide the smell of hot meat since. Why do your dogs bark so? be
there bears i' the town?

ANNE.   I think there are, sir; I heard them talked of.

SLEN.   I love the sport well; but I shall as soon quarrel at it as any man
in England. You are afraid, if you see the bear loose, are you not?

ANNE.   Ay, indeed, sir.

SLEN.   That's meat and drink[31] to me, now. I have seen Sackerson[32]
loose twenty times, and have taken him by the chain; but, I warrant you, the women have so cried and shrieked at it, that it
passed: but women, indeed, cannot abide 'em; they are very ill-
favoured rough things.

Re-enter PAGE

PAGE.   Come, gentle Master Slender, come; we stay for you.

SLEN.   I'll eat nothing, I thank you, sir.

PAGE.   By cock and pie, you shall not choose, sir! come, come.

SLEN.   Nay, pray you, lead the way.

PAGE.   Come on, sir.

SLEN.   Mistress Anne, yourself shall go first.

ANNE.   Not I, sir; pray you, keep on.

SLEN.   Truly, I will not go first; truly, la! I will not do you that wrong.

ANNE.   I pray you, sir.

SLEN.   I'll rather be unmannerly than troublesome. You do yourself
wrong, indeed, la!   [*Exeunt.*

---

[30]*three veneys . . . prunes*] The wager for which the fencing-match was played was a dish
of stewed prunes to be paid to him who scored three "veneys" (*i.e.* hits).

[31]*meat and drink*] a common proverbial phrase, expressing infinite satisfaction.

[32]*Sackerson*] The name of a far-famed performing bear, which was a chief attraction, at
the date of the performance of this play, at the Paris Garden in Southwark.

SCENE II. *The Same.*

Enter SIR HUGH EVANS *and* SIMPLE

EVANS.   Go your ways, and ask of Doctor Caius' house which is the
way: and there dwells one Mistress Quickly, which is in the manner of his nurse, or his dry nurse, or his cook, or his laundry, his
washer, and his wringer.

SIM.   Well, sir.

EVANS.   Nay, it is petter yet. Give her this letter; for it is a 'oman that
altogether's acquaintance[1] with Mistress Anne Page: and the letter
is, to desire and require her to solicit your master's desires to
Mistress Anne Page. I pray you, be gone: I will make an end of my
dinner; there's pippins and cheese to come.   [*Exeunt.*

SCENE III. *A Room in the Garter Inn.*

Enter FALSTAFF, Host, BARDOLPH, NYM, PISTOL, *and* ROBIN

FAL.   Mine host of the Garter!

HOST.   What say my bully-rook? speak scholarly and wisely.

FAL.   Truly, mine host, I must turn away some of my followers.

HOST.   Discard, bully Hercules; cashier: let them wag; trot, trot.

FAL.   I sit at ten pounds a week.

HOST.   Thou 'rt an emperor, Cæsar, Keisar, and Pheezar. I will entertain Bardolph; he shall draw, he shall tap: said I well, bully
Hector?

FAL.   Do so, good mine host.

HOST.   I have spoke; let him follow. [*To* BARD.] Let me see thee froth
and lime:[1] I am at a word; follow.   [*Exit.*

FAL.   Bardolph, follow him. A tapster is a good trade: an old cloak
makes a new jerkin; a withered serving-man a fresh tapster. Go;
adieu.

BARD.   It is a life that I have desired: I will thrive.

PIST.   O base Hungarian[2] wight! wilt thou the spigot wield?
                                                   [*Exit* BARDOLPH.

---

[1]*that altogether's acquaintance*] that is fully acquainted with.

[1]*froth and lime*] The host invites Bardolph to try his hand as a tapster, whose function
it was to make the beer "froth and lime," *i.e.* sparkle by covertly introducing *lime* into
the glass.

[2]*Hungarian*] The earlier Quartos read *Gongarian*. Steevens quoted without reference a
line from an unidentified old play, "O base Gongarian! wilt thou the distaff wield?" But
the epithet "Hungarian" was often used in the sense of "swaggering" or "bombastic."

NYM. He was gotten in drink: is not the humour conceited?

FAL. I am glad I am so acquit of this tinder-box: his thefts were too open; his filching was like an unskilful singer; he kept not time.

NYM. The good humour is to steal at a minute's rest.[3]

PIST. "Convey," the wise it call. "Steal!" foh! a fico for the phrase!

FAL. Well, sirs, I am almost out at heels.

PIST. Why, then, let kibes ensue.

FAL. There is no remedy; I must cony-catch; I must shift.

PIST. Young ravens must have food.

FAL. Which of you know Ford of this town?

PIST. I ken the wight: he is of substance good.

FAL. My honest lads, I will tell you what I am about.

PIST. Two yards, and more.

FAL. No quips now, Pistol! Indeed, I am in the waist two yards about; but I am now about no waste; I am about thrift. Briefly, I do mean to make love to Ford's wife: I spy entertainment in her; she discourses, she carves, she gives the leer of invitation: I can construe the action of her familiar style; and the hardest voice of her behaviour, to be Englished rightly, is "I am Sir John Falstaff's."

PIST. He hath studied her will, and translated her will,[4] out of honesty into English.

NYM. The anchor is deep: will that humour pass?

FAL. Now, the report goes she has all the rule of her husband's purse: he hath a legion of angels.

PIST. As many devils entertain; and "To her, boy," say I.

NYM. The humour rises; it is good: humour me the angels.

FAL. I have writ me here a letter to her: and here another to Page's wife, who even now gave me good eyes too, examined my parts with most judicious œillades;[5] sometimes the beam of her view gilded my foot, sometimes my portly belly.

PIST. Then did the sun on dunghill shine.

NYM. I thank thee for that humour.

FAL. O, she did so course o'er my exteriors with such a greedy intention, that the appetite of her eye did seem to scorch me up like a burning-glass! Here's another letter to her: she bears the purse too;

---

[3] *at a minute's rest*] This, the original reading, has been ingeniously altered by many editors to *at a minim's rest*. "Minim" is the shortest note in music. "At a minim's rest" would mean "with the utmost rapidity."

[4] *will . . . will*] This is the reading of the First Folio. The earlier Quartos read *well* for the first *will* and omit the second phrase. *Will* in both cases is doubtless right.

[5] *œillades*] A French word meaning "amorous glances," very occasionally met with in Elizabethan literature.

she is a region in Guiana,[6] all gold and bounty. I will be cheaters[7]
to them both, and they shall be exchequers to me; they shall be
my East and West Indies, and I will trade to them both. Go bear
thou this letter to Mistress Page; and thou this to Mistress Ford: we
will thrive, lads, we will thrive.

PIST.   Shall I sir Pandarus of Troy become,
And by my side wear steel? then, Lucifer take all!

NYM.   I will run no base humour: here, take the humour-letter: I will
keep the haviour of reputation.

FAL. [*To* ROBIN]   Hold, sirrah, bear you these letters tightly;
Sail like my pinnace to these golden shores.
Rogues, hence, avaunt! vanish like hailstones, go;
Trudge, plod away o' the hoof; seek shelter, pack!
Falstaff will learn the humour of the age,
French thrift, you rogues; myself and skirted page.

                                        [*Exeunt* FALSTAFF *and* ROBIN.

PIST.   Let vultures gripe thy guts! for gourd and fullam holds,
And high and low[8] beguiles the rich and poor:
Tester I'll have in pouch when thou shalt lack,
Base Phrygian Turk!

NYM.   I have operations which be humours of revenge.

PIST.   Wilt thou revenge?

NYM.   By welkin and her star!

PIST.   With wit or steel?

NYM.   With both the humours, I:
I will discuss the humour of this love to Page.

PIST.   And I to Ford shall eke unfold
        How Falstaff, varlet vile,
        His dove will prove, his gold will hold,
        And his soft couch defile.

NYM.   My humour shall not cool: I will incense Page to deal with
poison; I will possess him with yellowness,[9] for the revolt of mine[10]
is dangerous: that is my true humour.

---

[6]*a region in Guiana*] An allusion to Sir Walter Ralegh's recent exploration of Guiana,
  of which he published an account in 1595.

[7]*cheaters*] A punning quibble on "cheaters" and "escheaters," officers of the Exchequer.

[8]*gourd . . . low*] "Gourd," "fullam," "high [men]" and "low [men]" were all cant terms
  for loaded dice in common use by sharpers.

[9]*yellowness*] the traditional colour of jealousy.

[10]*revolt of mine*] This is the original reading. Theobald suggested *revolt of mien* (*i.e.*
  change of complexion), which does not add much point to Nym's threat. The
  Cambridge editors suggest that "anger" is omitted after "mine." Most probably Nym
  merely means to say in his grandiloquent jargon "my revolt," *i.e.* "my purpose of re-
  nouncing allegiance to Falstaff."

PIST.   Thou art the Mars of malecontents: I second thee; troop on.
                                                              [*Exeunt.*

SCENE IV. *A Room in Doctor Caius's House.*

Enter MISTRESS QUICKLY, SIMPLE, *and* RUGBY

QUICK.   What, John Rugby! I pray thee, go to the casement, and see
    if you can see my master, Master Doctor Caius, coming. If he do,
    i' faith, and find any body in the house, here will be an old abus-
    ing of God's patience and the king's English.
RUG.   I'll go watch.
QUICK.   Go; and we'll have a posset for 't soon at night, in faith, at the
    latter end of a sea-coal fire. [*Exit* RUGBY.] An honest, willing, kind
    fellow, as ever servant shall come in house withal; and, I warrant
    you, no tell-tale nor no breed-bate: his worst fault is, that he is
    given to prayer; he is something peevish that way: but nobody but
    has his fault; but let that pass. Peter Simple, you say your name is?
SIM.   Ay, for fault of a better.
QUICK.   And Master Slender's your master?
SIM.   Ay, forsooth.
QUICK.   Does he not wear a great round beard, like a glover's paring-
    knife?
SIM.   No, forsooth: he hath but a little wee face,[1] with a little yellow
    beard,—a Cain-coloured[2] beard.
QUICK.   A softly-sprighted man, is he not?
SIM.   Ay, forsooth: but he is as tall a man of his hands[3] as any is be-
    tween this and his head; he hath fought with a warrener.
QUICK.   How say you?—O, I should remember him: does he not hold
    up his head, as it were, and strut in his gait?
SIM.   Yes, indeed, does he.
QUICK.   Well, heaven send Anne Page no worse fortune! Tell Master

[1]*wee face*] This is the original reading. Capell needlessly substituted *whey-face* (meaning "pale-faced"), as in *Macb.*, V, iii. In the Second Quarto (in the preceding speech,
which the Folio alters), Dame Quickly applies to Slender's beard the epithet "whay
coloured," but *wee* is quite appropriate to the context.
[2]*Cain-coloured*] The early Quartos read "*Kane* colored," which tends to justify the popular emendation "*Cane*-coloured" for the First Folio reading "*Caine*-colored." "Cane-
coloured beard" would be much the same as "straw-colour beard" in *Mids. N. Dr.*, I,
ii. If "*Cain*-coloured" be retained, there would be a reference to the red colour of
Cain's beard in current pictorial illustrations of Scriptural history.
[3]*as tall a man of his hands*] In Florio's *Italian Dictionary*, 1598, "manesco" is inter-
preted as "readie or nimble-handed; *a tall man of his hands.*"

Parson Evans I will do what I can for your master: Anne is a good girl, and I wish—

Re-enter RUGBY

RUG.   Out, alas! here comes my master.
QUICK.   We shall all be shent. Run in here, good young man; go into this closet: he will not stay long. [*Shuts* SIMPLE *in the closet.*] What, John Rugby! John! what, John, I say! Go, John, go inquire for my master; I doubt he be not well, that he comes not home.

[*Singing*] And down, down, adown-a, &c.

Enter DOCTOR CAIUS

CAIUS.   Vat is you sing? I do not like des toys. Pray you, go and vetch me in my closet un boitier vert,—a box, a green-a box: do intend vat I speak? a green-a box.
QUICK.   Ay, forsooth; I'll fetch it you. [*Aside*] I am glad he went not in himself: if he had found the young man, he would have been horn-mad.
CAIUS.   Fe, fe, fe, fe! ma foi, il fait fort chaud. Je m'en vais à la cour,—la grande affaire.
QUICK.   Is it this, sir?
CAIUS.   Oui; mette le au mon pocket: dépêcne, quickly. Vere is dat knave Rugby?
QUICK.   What, John Rugby! John!
RUG.   Here, Sir!
CAIUS.   You are John Rugby, and you are Jack Rugby. Come, take-a your rapier, and come after my heel to the court.
RUG.   'T is ready, sir, here in the porch.
CAIUS.   By my trot, I tarry too long. Od's me! Qu'ai-j'oublié! dere is some simples in my closet, dat I vill not for the varld I shall leave behind.
QUICK.   Ay me, he'll find the young man there, and be mad!
CAIUS.   O diable, diable! vat is in my closet? Villain! larron! [*Pulling* SIMPLE *out.*] Rugby, my rapier!
QUICK.   Good master, be content.
CAIUS.   Wherefore shall I be content-a?
QUICK.   The young man is an honest man.
CAIUS.   What shall de honest man do in my closet? dere is no honest man dat shall come in my closet.
QUICK.   I beseech you, be not so phlegmatic. Here the truth of it: he came of an errand to me from Parson Hugh.
CAIUS.   Vell.
SIM.   Ay, forsooth; to desire her to—

QUICK.　Peace, I pray you.

CAIUS.　Peace-a your tongue. Speak-a your tale.

SIM.　To desire this honest gentlewoman, your maid, to speak a good
word to Mistress Anne Page for my master in the way of marriage.

QUICK.　This is all, indeed, la! but I'll ne'er put my finger in the fire,
and need not.

CAIUS.　Sir Hugh send-a you? Rugby, baille[4] me some paper. Tarry
you a little-a while.　　　　　　　　　　　　　　　　[*Writes.*

QUICK. [*Aside to* SIMPLE]　I am glad he is so quiet: if he had been
throughly moved, you should have heard him so loud and so
melancholy. But notwithstanding, man, I'll do you your master
what good I can: and the very yea and the no is, the French doctor, my master,—I may call him my master, look you, for I keep
his house; and I wash, wring, brew, bake, scour, dress meat and
drink, make the beds, and do all myself,—

SIM. [*Aside to* QUICKLY]　'T is a great charge to come under one body's
hand.

QUICK. [*Aside to* SIMPLE]　Are you avised o' that? you shall find it a
great charge: and to be up early and down late;—but notwithstanding,—to tell you in your ear; I would have no words of it,—
my master himself is in love with Mistress Anne Page: but notwithstanding that, I know Anne's mind,—that's neither here nor there.

CAIUS.　You jack'nape, give-a this letter to Sir Hugh; by gar, it is a shal-
lenge: I will cut his troat in de park; and I will teach a scurvy jack-
a-nape priest to meddle or make. You may be gone; it is not good
you tarry here.—By gar, I will cut all his two stones; by gar, he
shall not have a stone to throw at his dog.　　　　[*Exit* SIMPLE.

QUICK.　Alas, he speaks but for his friends.

CAIUS.　It is no matter-a ver dat:—do not you tell-a me dat I shall have
Anne Page for myself?—By gar, I vill kill de Jack priest; and I have
appointed mine host of de Jarteer to measure our weapon.—By
gar, I will myself have Anne Page.

QUICK.　Sir, the maid loves you, and all shall be well. We must give
folks leave to prate: what, the good-jer![5]

CAIUS.　Rugby, come to the court with me. By gar, if I have not Anne
Page, I shall turn your head out of my door. Follow my heels,
Rugby.　　　　　　　　　　　　　　[*Exeunt* CAIUS *and* RUGBY.

QUICK.　You shall have An fool's-head of your own.[6] No, I know
Anne's mind for that: never a woman in Windsor knows more of

---

[4]*baille*] French for "give, deliver."

[5]*what, the good-jer!*] a common expletive expressive of surprise; "in the name of fortune!"

[6]*fool's-head . . . own*] make a fool of yourself.

Anne's mind than I do; nor can do more than I do with her, I thank heaven.

FENT. [*Within*]   Who's within there? ho!

QUICK.   Who's there, I trow? Come near the house, I pray you.

Enter FENTON

FENT.   How now, good woman! how dost thou?

QUICK.   The better that it pleases your good worship to ask.

FENT.   What news? how does pretty Mistress Anne?

QUICK.   In truth, sir, and she is pretty, and honest, and gentle; and one that is your friend, I can tell you that by the way; I praise heaven for it.

FENT.   Shall I do any good, think'st thou? shall I not lose my suit?

QUICK.   Troth, sir, all is in his hands above: but notwithstanding, Master Fenton, I'll be sworn on a book, she loves you. Have not your worship a wart above your eye?

FENT.   Yes, marry, have I; what of that?

QUICK.   Well, thereby hangs a tale:—good faith, it is such another Nan; but, I detest, an honest maid as ever broke bread:—we had an hour's talk of that wart.—I shall never laugh but in that maid's company!—But, indeed, she is given too much to allicholy and musing: but for you—well, go to.

FENT.   Well, I shall see her to-day. Hold, there's money for thee; let me have thy voice in my behalf: if thou seest her before me, commend me.

QUICK.   Will I? i' faith, that we will; and I will tell your worship more of the wart the next time we have confidence; and of other wooers.

FENT.   Well, farewell; I am in great haste now.

QUICK.   Farewell to your worship. [*Exit* FENTON.] Truly, an honest gentleman: but Anne loves him not; for I know Anne's mind as well as another does.—Out upon 't! what have I forgot?   [*Exit.*

ACT II.

Scene I. *Before Page's House.*

Enter Mistress Page, *with a letter*

Mistress Page.   What, have I scaped love-letters in the holiday-time
of my beauty, and am I now a subject for them? Let me see.
                                                            [*Reads.*

"Ask me no reason why I love you; for though Love use Reason for his
physician, he admits him not for his counsellor. You are not young, no
more am I; go to, then, there's sympathy: you are merry, so am I; ha, ha!
then there's more sympathy: you love sack, and so do I; would you desire
better sympathy? Let it suffice thee, Mistress Page,—at the least, if the
love of soldier can suffice,—that I love thee. I will not say, pity me,—'t
is not a soldier-like phrase; but I say, love me. By me,

              Thine own true knight,
              By day or night,
              Or any kind of light,
              With all his might
              For thee to fight,   John Falstaff."

What a herod of Jewry is this! O wicked, wicked world! One that
is well-nigh worn to pieces with age to show himself a young gallant! What an unweighed behaviour hath this Flemish drunkard
picked—with the devil's name!—out of my conversation, that he
dares in this manner assay me? Why, he hath not been thrice in
my company! What should I say to him? I was then frugal of my
mirth: Heaven forgive me! Why, I'll exhibit a bill in the parlia-
ment for the putting down of men. How shall I be revenged
on him? for revenged I will be, as sure as his guts are made of
puddings.

Enter Mistress Ford

Mrs Ford.   Mistress Page! trust me, I was going to your house.

16

MRS PAGE.   And, trust me, I was coming to you. You look very ill.

MRS FORD.   Nay, I'll ne'er believe that; I have to show to the contrary.

MRS PAGE.   Faith, but you do, in my mind.

MRS FORD.   Well, I do, then; yet, I say, I could show you to the contrary. O Mistress Page, give me some counsel!

MRS PAGE.   What's the matter, woman?

MRS FORD.   O woman, if it were not for one trifling respect, I could come to such honour!

MRS PAGE.   Hang the trifle, woman! take the honour. What is it?—dispense with trifles;—what is it?

MRS FORD.   If I would but go to hell for an eternal moment or so, I could be knighted.

MRS PAGE.   What? thou liest! Sir Alice Ford! These knights will hack;[1] and so thou shouldst not alter the article of thy gentry.

MRS FORD.   We burn daylight:[2]—here, read, read; perceive how I might be knighted. I shall think the worse of fat men, as long as I have an eye to make difference of men's liking: and yet he would not swear; praised women's modesty; and gave such orderly and well-behaved reproof to all uncomeliness, that I would have sworn his disposition would have gone to the truth of his words; but they do no more adhere and keep place together than the Hundredth Psalm to the tune of "Green Sleeves."[3] What tempest, I trow, threw this whale, with so many tuns of oil in his belly, ashore at Windsor? How shall I be revenged on him? I think the best way were to entertain him with hope, till the wicked fire of lust have melted him in his own grease. Did you ever hear the like?

MRS PAGE.   Letter for letter, but that the name of Page and Ford differs! To thy great comfort in this mystery of ill opinions, here's the twin-brother of thy letter: but let thine inherit first; for, I protest,

---

[1]*hack*] commonly explained in the unsupported sense of "grow hackneyed," "pall," "get too common," with a reference to James I's indiscriminate creation of knights (at a date later than the first draft of the play). There seems no point in the suggestion that "hack" is used here in its ordinary sense of "mutilate," "cut off," in allusion to the ceremonial degradation of unworthy knights by cutting off their spurs, the special emblem of chivalry. "Hack" undoubtedly appears in its ordinary sense of "mutilate," *infra*, III, i, but in a later scene it recurs in quite a different and apparently a ribald sense in IV, i, where Mrs. Quickly says a boy is taught by his master "*to hick and to hack*, which they'll do fast enough of themselves, and to call 'horum' (*i.e.* whore)." "Hack" or "hackney" was a slang name for a loose woman, and hence a verb meaning "to have dealings with loose women" is deducible. It is possible that Mrs. Page here intends some such quibbling allusion.

[2]*We burn daylight*] to lose time.

[3]*the tune of "Green Sleeves"*] One of the most popular ballads of Shakespeare's day.

mine never shall. I warrant he hath a thousand of these letters, writ with blank space for different names,—sure, more,—and these are of the second edition: he will print them, out of doubt; for he cares not what he puts into the press, when he would put us two. I had rather be a giantess, and lie under Mount Pelion. Well, I will find you twenty lascivious turtles ere one chaste man.

MRS FORD.   Why, this is the very same; the very hand, the very words. What doth he think of us?

MRS PAGE.   Nay, I know not: it makes me almost ready to wrangle with mine own honesty. I'll entertain myself like one that I am not acquainted withal; for, sure, unless he know some strain[4] in me, that I know not myself, he would never have boarded me in this fury.

MRS FORD.   "Boarding," call you it? I'll be sure to keep him above deck.

MRS PAGE.   So will I: if he come under my hatches, I'll never to sea again. Let's be revenged on him: let's appoint him a meeting; give him a show of comfort in his suit, and lead him on with a fine-baited delay, till he hath pawned his horses to mine host of the Garter.

MRS FORD.   Nay, I will consent to act any villany against him, that may not sully the chariness of our honesty. O, that my husband saw this letter! it would give eternal food to his jealousy.

MRS PAGE.   Why, look where he comes; and my good man too: he's as far from jealousy as I am from giving him cause; and that, I hope, is an unmeasurable distance.

MRS FORD.   You are the happier woman.

MRS PAGE.   Let's consult together against this greasy knight. Come hither.   [*They retire.*

Enter FORD, *with* PISTOL, *and* PAGE, *with* NYM

FORD.   Well, I hope it be not so.

PIST.   Hope is a curtal dog in some affairs:
    Sir John affects thy wife.

FORD.   Why, sir, my wife is not young.

PIST.   He wooes both high and low, both rich and poor,
    Both young and old, one with another, Ford;
    He loves the gallimaufry:[5] Ford, perpend.

FORD.   Love my wife!

[4]*some strain*] some natural disposition (to sensuality).
[5]*gallimaufry*] This word, which is from the French, properly means "a stew or hash" of mixed meats. Pistol applies it to a promiscuous assembly of persons.

PIST.   With liver burning hot. Prevent, or go thou,
    Like Sir Actæon he, with Ringwood[6] at thy heels:
    O, odious is the name!

FORD.   What name, sir?

PIST.   The horn, I say. Farewell.
    Take heed; have open eye; for thieves do foot by night:
    Take heed, ere summer comes, or cuckoo-birds do sing.
    Away, Sir Corporal Nym!—
    Believe it, Page; he speaks sense.   [*Exit.*

FORD. [*Aside*]   I will be patient; I will find out this.

NYM. [*To* PAGE]   And this is true; I like not the humour of lying. He
hath wronged me in some humours: I should have borne the hu-
moured letter to her; but I have a sword, and it shall bite upon my
necessity. He loves your wife; there's the short and the long. My
name is Corporal Nym; I speak, and I avouch; 't is true: my name
is Nym, and Falstaff loves your wife. Adieu. I love not the humour
of bread and cheese; and there's the humour of it. Adieu.   [*Exit.*

PAGE.   "The humour of it," quoth 'a! here's a fellow frights English out
of his wits.

FORD.   I will seek out Falstaff.

PAGE.   I never heard such a drawling, affecting rogue.

FORD.   If I do find it:—well.

PAGE.   I will not believe such a Cataian,[7] though the priest o' the town
commended him for a true man.

FORD.   'T was a good sensible fellow:—well.

PAGE.   How now, Meg!

                         [MRS PAGE *and* MRS FORD *come forward.*

MRS PAGE.   Whither go you, George? Hark you.

MRS FORD.   How now, sweet Frank! why art thou melancholy?

FORD.   I melancholy! I am not melancholy. Get you home, go.

MRS FORD.   Faith, thou hast some crotchets in thy head. Now, will
you go, Mistress Page?

MRS PAGE.   Have with you. You'll come to dinner, George? [*Aside to*
MRS FORD] Look who comes yonder: she shall be our messenger
to this paltry knight.

MRS FORD. [*Aside to* MRS PAGE]   Trust me, I thought on her: she'll fit
it.

---

[6]*Sir Actæon . . . Ringwood*] The story of Actæon, an ardent hunter, who for defying
Diana, goddess of the chase, was turned by her into a stag, is told by Ovid. Ovid gives
the names of Actæon's hounds, the last being called "Hylactor." Golding, in his trans-
lation of Ovid's *Metamorphoses*, renders the name "Hylactor" by "*Ringwood*." This is
clear proof of Shakespeare's indebtedness to Golding in this passage. Actæon's transformation to a horned stag is noticed below, III, ii: "a secure and wilful *Actæon*."

[7]*Cataian*] Literally, a native of Cathay or China, but often used for "thief" or "sharper."

Enter MISTRESS QUICKLY

MRS PAGE.   You are come to see my daughter Anne?

QUICK.   Ay, forsooth; and, I pray, how does good Mistress Anne?

MRS PAGE.   Go in with us and see: we have an hour's talk with you.

          [*Exeunt* MRS PAGE, MRS FORD, *and* MRS QUICKLY.

PAGE.   How now, Master Ford!

FORD.   You heard what this knave told me, did you not?

PAGE.   Yes: and you heard what the other told me?

FORD.   Do you think there is truth in them?

PAGE.   Hang 'em, slaves! I do not think the knight would offer it: but these that accuse him in his intent towards our wives are a yoke of his discarded men; very rogues, now they be out of service.

FORD.   Were they his men?

PAGE.   Marry, were they.

FORD.   I like it never the better for that. Does he lie at the Garter?

PAGE.   Ay, marry, does he. If he should intend this voyage toward my wife, I would turn her loose to him; and what he gets more of her than sharp words, let it lie on my head.

FORD.   I do not misdoubt my wife; but I would be loath to turn them together. A man may be too confident: I would have nothing lie on my head: I cannot be thus satisfied.

PAGE.   Look where my ranting host of the Garter comes: there is either liquor in his pate, or money in his purse, when he looks so merrily.

Enter HOST

     How now, mine host!

HOST.   How now, bully-rook! thou 'rt a gentleman. Cavaleiro-justice, I say!

Enter SHALLOW

SHAL.   I follow, mine host, I follow. Good even and twenty, good Master Page! Master Page, will you go with us? we have sport in hand.

HOST.   Tell him, cavaleiro-justice; tell him, bully-rook.

SHAL.   Sir, there is a fray to be fought between Sir Hugh the Welsh priest and Caius the French doctor.

FORD.   Good mine host o' the Garter, a word with you.

          [*Drawing him aside.*

HOST.   What say'st thou, my bully-rook?

SHAL. [*To* PAGE]   Will you go with us to behold it? My merry host hath had the measuring of their weapons; and, I think, hath appointed

them contrary places; for, believe me, I hear the parson is no
jester. Hark, I will tell you what our sport shall be.

[They converse apart.

HOST.   Hast thou no suit against my knight, my guest-cavaleire?

FORD.   None, I protest: but I'll give you a pottle of burnt sack[8] to give
me recourse to him, and tell him my name is Brook; only for a
jest.

HOST.   My hand, bully; thou shalt have egress and regress;—said I
well?—and thy name shall be Brook. It is a merry knight. Will you
go, An-heires?[9]

SHAL.   Have with you, mine host.

PAGE.   I have heard the Frenchman hath good skill in his rapier.

SHAL.   Tut, sir, I could have told you more. In these times you stand
on distance, your passes, stoccadoes, and I know not what: 't is the
heart, Master Page; 't is here, 't is here. I have seen the time, with
my long sword I would have made you four tall fellows skip like
rats.

HOST.   Here, boys, here, here! shall we wag?

PAGE.   Have with you. I had rather hear them scold than fight.

[Exeunt HOST, SHAL., *and* PAGE.

FORD.   Though Page be a secure fool, and stands so firmly on his
wife's frailty,[10] yet I cannot put off my opinion so easily: she was in
his company at Page's house; and what they made there, I know
not. Well, I will look further into 't: and I have a disguise to sound
Falstaff. If I find her honest, I lose not my labour; if she be otherwise, 't is labour well bestowed.   *[Exit.*

SCENE II. *A Room in The Garter Inn.*

Enter FALSTAFF *and* PISTOL

FAL.   I will not lend thee a penny.

PIST.   Why, then the world 's mine oyster,
    Which I with sword will open.

[8]*burnt sack*] apparently sack heated by dipping a red-hot iron in the liquid.

[9]*An-heires*] This is the reading of the early editions, and is an obvious misprint.
Theobald substituted *myn-heers* (*i.e.* the Dutch word for "gentlemen," which was not
unfamiliar in colloquial English). It seems more probable that the host used the word
"hearts" or "my hearts," *i.e.* brave fellows. This is the host's greeting in like circum-
stances, III, ii, *infra* ("Farewell, my *hearts*").

[10]*stands . . . frailty*] Malone explains "has such perfect confidence in his unchaste wife,"
Ford being supposed to credit every woman with frailty. Theobald read *fealty* for
frailty, and thus removed the ambiguity, which was probably intentional on the author's part.

FAL.   Not a penny. I have been content, sir, you should lay my coun-
tenance to pawn: I have grated upon[1] my good friends for three re-
prieves for you and your coach-fellow Nym; or else you had
looked through the grate,[2] like a geminy of baboons. I am damned
in hell for swearing to gentlemen my friends, you were good sol-
diers and tall fellows; and when Mistress Bridget lost the handle of
her fan, I took 't upon mine honour thou hadst it not.

PIST.   Didst not thou share? hadst thou not fifteen pence?

FAL.   Reason, you rogue, reason: think'st thou I'll endanger my soul
gratis? At a word, hang no more about me, I am no gibbet for you.
Go. A short knife and a throng![3] — To your manor of Pickt-hatch![4]
Go. You'll not bear a letter for me, you rogue! you stand upon
your honour! Why, thou unconfinable baseness, it is as much as I
can do to keep the terms of my honour precise: I, I, I myself sometimes, leaving the fear of God on the left hand, and hiding mine
honour in my necessity, am fain to shuffle, to hedge, and to lurch;
and yet you, rogue, will ensconce your rags, your cat-a-mountain
looks, your red-lattice phrases,[5] and your bold-beating[6] oaths,
under the shelter of your honour! You will not do it, you!

PIST.   I do relent: what would thou more of man?

Enter ROBIN

ROB.   Sir, here's a woman would speak with you.
FAL.   Let her approach.

Enter MISTRESS QUICKLY

QUICK.   Give your worship good morrow.
FAL.   Good morrow, good wife.
QUICK.   Not so, an 't please your worship.
FAL.   Good maid, then.
QUICK.   I'll be sworn;
      As my mother was, the first hour I was born.
FAL.   I do believe the swearer. What with me?

---

[1]*grated upon*] worried, annoyed.

[2]*through the grate*] sc. of the prison cell.

[3]*A short knife . . . throng*] Falstaff ironically recommends the short knife which cut-
purses were wont to turn to account in a throng or crowd.

[4]*Pickt-hatch*] The name of a street in Clerkenwell, London, which was notoriously fre-
quented by loose characters. The name seems to mean a hatch (*i.e.* wicket, gate, half
door) with pikes or spikes fastened at the top. Some of the houses in the street were
thus distinguished.

[5]*red-lattice phrases*] tavern parlour talk.

[6]*bold-beating*] hectoring, braggadocio-like. For this, the original reading, Hanmer ingeniously suggested *bull-baiting*.

QUICK.   Shall I vouchsafe your worship a word or two?

FAL.   Two thousand, fair woman: and I'll vouchsafe thee the hearing.

QUICK.   There is one Mistress Ford, sir:—I pray, come a little nearer this ways:—I myself dwell with Master Doctor Caius,—

FAL.   Well, on: Mistress Ford, you say,—

QUICK.   Your worship says very true:—I pray your worship, come a little nearer this ways.

FAL.   I warrant thee, nobody hears;—mine own people, mine own people.

QUICK.   Are they so? God bless them, and make them his servants!

FAL.   Well, Mistress Ford;—what of her?

QUICK.   Why, sir, she's a good creature.—Lord, Lord! your worship's a wanton! Well, heaven forgive you and all of us, I pray!

FAL.   Mistress Ford;—come, Mistress Ford,—

QUICK.   Marry, this is the short and the long of it; you have brought her into such a canaries[7] as 't is wonderful. The best courtier of them all, when the court lay at Windsor, could never have brought her to such a canary. Yet there has been knights, and lords, and gentlemen, with their coaches; I warrant you, coach after coach, letter after letter, gift after gift; smelling so sweetly, all musk, and so rushling, I warrant you, in silk and gold; and in such alligant terms; and in such wine and sugar of the best and the fairest, that would have won any woman's heart; and, I warrant you, they could never get an eye-wink of her: I had myself twenty angels given me this morning; but I defy all angels—in any such sort, as they say—but in the way of honesty: and, I warrant you, they could never get her so much as sip on a cup with the proudest of them all: and yet there has been earls, nay, which is more, pensioners;[8] but, I warrant you, all is one with her.

FAL.   But what says she to me? be brief, my good she-Mercury.

QUICK.   Marry, she hath received your letter; for the which she thanks you a thousand times; and she gives you to notify, that her husband will be absence from his house between ten and eleven.

FAL.   Ten and eleven.

QUICK.   Ay, forsooth; and then you may come and see the picture, she says, that you wot of: Master Ford, her husband, will be from home. Alas, the sweet woman leads an ill life with him! he's a very jealousy man: she leads a very frampold life with him, good heart.

FAL.   Ten and eleven. Woman, commend me to her; I will not fail her.

[7]*canaries*] a dance with a very quick step. Mrs. Quickly confused the word with "quandary."

[8]*pensioners*] gentlemen of the sovereign's body guard.

QUICK.   Why, you say well. But I have another messenger to your worship. Mistress Page hath her hearty commendations to you, too:
and let me tell you in your ear, she's as fartuous a civil modest
wife, and one, I tell you, that will not miss you morning nor
evening prayer, as any is in Windsor, whoe'er be the other: and
she bade me tell your worship that her husband is seldom from
home; but, she hopes, there will come a time. I never knew a
woman so dote upon a man: surely, I think you have charms, la;
yes, in truth.

FAL.   Not I, I assure thee: setting the attraction of my good parts aside,
I have no other charms.

QUICK.   Blessing on your heart for 't!

FAL.   But, I pray thee, tell me this: has Ford's wife and Page's wife acquainted each other how they love me?

QUICK.   That were a jest indeed! they have not so little grace, I hope:
that were a trick indeed! But Mistress Page would desire you to
send her your little page, of all loves:[9] her husband has a marvel-
lous infection to the little page; and, truly, Master Page is an honest man. Never a wife in Windsor leads a better life than she does:
do what she will, say what she will, take all, pay all, go to bed when
she list, rise when she list, all is as she will: and, truly, she deserves
it; for if there be a kind woman in Windsor, she is one. You must
send her your page; no remedy.

FAL.   Why, I will.

QUICK.   Nay, but do so, then: and, look you, he may come and go between you both; and, in any case, have a nay-word,[10] that you may
know one another's mind, and the boy never need to understand
any thing; for 't is not good that children should know any wicked-
ness: old folks, you know, have discretion, as they say, and know
the world.

FAL.   Fare thee well: commend me to them both: there's my purse; I
am yet thy debtor. Boy, go along with this woman. [*Exeunt*
MISTRESS QUICKLY *and* ROBIN.] This news distracts me!

PIST.   This punk is one of Cupid's carriers:
Clap on more sails; pursue; up with your fights:[11]
Give fire: she is my prize, or ocean whelm them all!   [*Exit.*

FAL.   Say'st thou so, old Jack? go thy ways; I'll make more of thy old
body than I have done. Will they yet look after thee? Wilt thou,

---

[9]*of all loves*] In *Othello*, III, i, the Quarto reading, "Desire you *of all loves*," is altered
in the Folios to *for loves sake*, the obvious meaning of the very common expression.
[10]*nay-word*] pass word.
[11]*fights*] "fighting sails," or screens which were hung round the decks of ships in action;
a technical term in nautical treatises.

after the expense of so much money, be now a gainer? Good body, I thank thee. Let them say 't is grossly done; so it be fairly done, no matter.

Enter BARDOLPH

BARD.   Sir John, there's one Master Brook below would fain speak with you, and be acquainted with you; and hath sent your worship a morning's draught of sack.

FAL.   Brook is his name?

BARD.   Ay, sir.

FAL.   Call him in. [*Exit* BARDOLPH.] Such Brooks are welcome to me, that o'erflow such liquor. Ah, ha! Mistress Ford and Mistress Page, have I encompassed you? go to; via!

Re-enter BARDOLPH, *with* FORD *disguised*

FORD.   Bless you, sir!

FAL.   And you, sir! Would you speak with me?

FORD.   I make bold to press with so little preparation upon you.

FAL.   You're welcome. What's your will?—Give us leave, drawer.
                                                          [*Exit* BARDOLPH.

FORD.   Sir, I am a gentleman that have spent much; my name is Brook.

FAL.   Good Master Brook, I desire more acquaintance of you.

FORD.   Good Sir John, I sue for yours: not to charge you; for I must let you understand I think myself in better plight for a lender than you are: the which hath something emboldened me to this unseasoned intrusion; for they say, if money go before, all ways do lie open.

FAL.   Money is a good soldier, sir, and will on.

FORD.   Troth, and I have a bag of money here troubles me: if you will help to bear it, Sir John, take all, or half, for easing me of the carriage.

FAL.   Sir, I know not how I may deserve to be your porter.

FORD.   I will tell you, sir, if you will give me the hearing.

FAL.   Speak, good Master Brook: I shall be glad to be your servant.

FORD.   Sir, I hear you are a scholar,—I will be brief with you,—and you have been a man long known to me, though I had never so good means, as desire, to make myself acquainted with you. I shall discover a thing to you, wherein I must very much lay open mine own imperfection: but, good Sir John, as you have one eye upon my follies, as you hear them unfolded, turn another into the register of your own; that I may pass with a reproof the easier, sith you yourself know how easy it is to be such an offender.

FAL. Very well, sir; proceed.

FORD. There is a gentlewoman in this town; her husband's name is Ford.

FAL. Well, sir.

FORD. I have long loved her, and, I protest to you, bestowed much on her; followed her with a doting observance; engrossed opportunities to meet her, fee'd every slight occasion that could but niggardly give me sight of her; not only bought many presents to give her, but have given largely to many to know what she would have given; briefly, I have pursued her as love hath pursued me; which hath been on the wing of all occasions. But whatsoever I have merited, either in my mind or in my means, meed, I am sure, I have received none; unless experience be a jewel that I have purchased at an infinite rate, and that hath taught me to say this:

"Love like a shadow flies when substance love pursues;
Pursuing that that flies, and flying what pursues."

FAL. Have you received no promise of satisfaction at her hands?

FORD. Never.

FAL. Have you importuned her to such a purpose?

FORD. Never.

FAL. Of what quality was your love, then?

FORD. Like a fair house built on another man's ground; so that I have lost my edifice by mistaking the place where I erected it.

FAL. To what purpose have you unfolded this to me?

FORD. When I have told you that, I have told you all. Some say, that though she appear honest to me, yet in other places she enlargeth her mirth so far that there is shrewd construction made of her. Now, Sir John, here is the heart of my purpose: you are a gentleman of excellent breeding, admirable discourse, of great admittance, authentic in your place and person, generally allowed[12] for your many war-like, court-like, and learned preparations.

FAL. O, sir!

FORD. Believe it, for you know it. There is money; spend it, spent it; spend more; spend all I have; only give me so much of your time in exchange of it, as to lay an amiable siege to the honesty of this Ford's wife: use your art of wooing; win her to consent to you: if any man may, you may as soon as any.

FAL. Would it apply well to the vehemency of your affection, that I

---

[12]*of great admittance . . . allowed*] being admitted into or fitted for great society, holding a position of recognized authority and importance, and being generally allowed or commended, etc.

should win what you would enjoy? Methinks you prescribe to
yourself very preposterously.

FORD.   O, understand my drift. She dwells so securely on the excellency of her honour, that the folly of my soul dares not present itself: she is too bright to be looked against. Now, could I come to
her with any detection in my hand, my desires had instance and
argument to commend themselves: I could drive her then from
the ward of her purity, her reputation, her marriage-vow, and a
thousand other her defences, which now are too too strongly em-
battled against me. What say you to 't, Sir John?

FAL.   Master Brook, I will first make bold with your money; next, give
me your hand; and last, as I am a gentleman, you shall, if you will,
enjoy Ford's wife.

FORD.   O good sir!

FAL.   I say you shall.

FORD.   Want no money, Sir John; you shall want none.

FAL.   Want no Mistress Ford, Master Brook; you shall want none. I
shall be with her, I may tell you, by her own appointment; even as
you came in to me, her assistant, or go-between, parted from me:
I say I shall be with her between ten and eleven; for at that time
the jealous rascally knave her husband will be forth. Come you to
me at night; you shall know how I speed.

FORD.   I am blest in your acquaintance. Do you know Ford, sir?

FAL.   Hang him, poor cuckoldly knave! I know him not:—yet I wrong
him to call him poor; they say the jealous wittolly knave hath
masses of money; for the which his wife seems to me well-
favoured. I will use her as the key of the cuckoldly rogue's coffer;
and there's my harvest-home.

FORD.   I would you knew Ford, sir, that you might avoid him, if you
saw him.

FAL.   Hang him, mechanical salt-butter rogue![13] I will stare him out
of his wits; I will awe him with my cudgel: it shall hang like a me-
teor o'er the cuckold's horns. Master Brook, thou shalt know I will
predominate over the peasant, and thou shalt lie with his wife.
Come to me soon at night. Ford's a knave, and I will aggravate his
style;[14] thou, Master Brook, shalt know him for knave and cuckold. Come to me soon at night.   [Exit.

FORD.   What a damned Epicurean rascal is this! My heart is ready to
crack with impatience. Who says this is improvident jealousy? my
wife hath sent to him; the hour is fixed; the match is made. Would

---

[13]*mechanical salt-butter rogue*] an artisan, who never tasted anything but salt butter.
[14]*aggravate his style*] add more titles (*i.e.* "knave" and "cuckold") to those he already
enjoys.

any man have thought this? See the hell of having a false woman! My bed shall be abused, my coffers ransacked, my reputation gnawn at; and I shall not only receive this villanous wrong, but stand under the adoption of abominable terms, and by him that does me this wrong. Terms! names!—Amaimon[15] sounds well; Lucifer, well; Barbason,[16] well; yet they are devils' additions, the names of fiends: but Cuckold! Wittol!—Cuckold! the devil himself hath not such a name. Page is an ass, a secure ass: he will trust his wife; he will not be jealous. I will rather trust a Fleming with my butter, Parson Hugh the Welshman with my cheese, an Irishman with my aqua-vitæ[17] bottle, or a thief to walk my ambling gelding, than my wife with herself: then she plots, then she ruminates, then she devises; and what they think in their hearts they may effect, they will break their hearts but they will effect. God be praised for my jealousy!—Eleven o'clock the hour. I will prevent this, detect my wife, be revenged on Falstaff, and laugh at Page. I will about it; better three hours too soon than a minute too late. Fie, fie, fie! cuckold! cuckold! cuckold!   [*Exit.*

Scene III. A *Field Near Windsor.*

Enter Caius *and* Rugby

Caius.   Jack Rugby!

Rug.   Sir?

Caius.   Vat is de clock, Jack?

Rug.   'T is past the hour, sir, that Sir Hugh promised to meet.

Caius.   By gar, he has save his soul, dat he is no come; he has pray his Pible well, dat he is no come: by gar, Jack Rugby, he is dead already, if he be come.

Rug.   He is wise, sir; he knew your worship would kill him, if he came.

Caius.   By gar, de herring is no dead so as I vill kill him. Take your rapier, Jack; I vill tell you how I vill kill him.

Rug.   Alas, sir, I cannot fence.

Caius.   Villainy, take your rapier.

Rug.   Forbear; here's company.

---

[15]*Amaimon*] The name of a demon or sprite, which figures in Reginald Scot's *Discovery of Witchcraft.*

[16]*Barbason*] represents Scot's fiend of hell called "Barbatos."

[17]*aqua-vitæ*] Usquebaugh, strong spirits, with indulgence in which Irishmen were commonly credited.

Enter HOST, SHALLOW, SLENDER, *and* PAGE

HOST.   Bless thee, bully doctor!

SHAL.   Save you, Master Doctor Gaius!

PAGE.   Now, good master doctor!

SLEN.   Give you good morrow, sir.

CAIUS.   Vat be all you, one, two, tree, four, come for?

HOST.   To see thee fight, to see thee foin, to see thee traverse; to see thee here, to see thee there; to see thee pass thy punto, thy stock, thy reverse, thy distance, thy montant.[1] Is he dead, my Ethiopian? is he dead, my Francisco? ha, bully! What says my Æsculapius? my Galen? my heart of elder?[2] ha! is he dead, bully-stale? is he dead?

CAIUS.   By gar, he is de coward Jack priest of de vorld; he is not show his face.

HOST.   Thou art a Castalion-King-Urinal.[3] Hector of Greece, my boy!

CAIUS.   I pray you, bear vitness that me have stay six or seven, two, tree hours for him, and he is no come.

SHAL.   He is the wiser man, master doctor: he is a curer of souls, and you a curer of bodies; if you should fight, you go against the hair of your professions. Is it not true, Master Page?

PAGE.   Master Shallow, you have yourself been a great fighter, though now a man of peace.

SHAL.   Bodykins, Master Page, though I now be old, and of the peace, if I see a sword out, my finger itches to make one. Though we are justices, and doctors, and churchmen, Master Page, we have some salt of our youth in us; we are the sons of women, Master Page.

PAGE.   'T is true, Master Shallow.

SHAL.   It will be found so, Master Page. Master Doctor Caius, I am come to fetch you home. I am sworn of the peace: you have shewed yourself a wise physician, and Sir Hugh hath shewn himself a wise and patient churchman. You must go with me, master doctor.

HOST.   Pardon, guest-justice.—A word, Mounseur Mock-water.

---

[1]*to see . . . montant*] Mine Host rattles off a long series of fencing terms. Thus "foin" is to "thrust"; "traverse" is to "parry"; "punto" and "stock" *i.e.* stoccato, both mean "thrust"; "reverse" is a backhanded stroke; "distance" is the space between the antagonists; "montant," or "montanto," is a direct blow.

[2]*my heart of elder*] a burlesque parody of "heart of oak"; the elder-tree's heart is of pith.

[3]*Castalion-King-Urinal*] This is the reading of the Folios. But the meaning is improved by the commonly accepted change, *Castilian, King-urinal!* "Castilian" was an epithet commonly applied to a braggadocio. In vulgar talk Elizabethan doctors were often jeered at for their professional practice of inspecting urine. The like intention is apparent in the host's insolent exclamations "bully-stale" and "Mock water" *i.e.* "Muck-water."

CAIUS.   Mock-vater! vat is dat?

HOST.   Mock-water, in our English tongue, is valour, bully.

CAIUS.   By gar, den, I have as much mock-vater as de Englishman.— Scurvy jack-dog priest! by gar, me vill cut his ears.

HOST.   He will clapper-claw thee tightly, bully.

CAIUS.   Clapper-de-claw! vat is dat?

HOST.   That is, he will make thee amends.

CAIUS.   By gar, me do look he shall clapper-de-claw me; for, by gar, me vill have it.

HOST.   And I will provoke him to 't, or let him wag.

CAIUS.   Me tank you for dat.

HOST.   And, moreover, bully,—But first, master guest, and Master Page, and eke Cavaleiro Slender, go you through the town to Frogmore.   [*Aside to them.*

PAGE.   Sir Hugh is there, is he?

HOST.   He is there: see what humour he is in; and I will bring the doctor about by the fields. Will it do well?

SHAL.   We will do it.

PAGE, SHAL., and SLEN.   Adieu, good master doctor.

[*Exeunt* PAGE, SHAL., *and* SLEN.

CAIUS.   By gar, me vill kill de priest; for he speak for a jack-an-ape to Anne Page.

HOST.   Let him die: sheathe thy impatience, throw cold water on thy choler: go about the fields with me through Frogmore: I will bring thee where Mistress Anne Page is, at a farm-house a-feasting; and thou shalt woo her. Cried I aim?[4] said I well?

CAIUS.   By gar, me dank you vor dat: by gar, I love you; and I shall procure-a you de good guest, de earl, de knight, de lords, de gentlemen, my patients.

HOST.   For the which I will be thy adversary toward Anne Page. Said I well?

CAIUS.   By gar, 't is good; vell said.

HOST.   Let us wag, then.

CAIUS.   Come at my heels, Jack Rugby.   [*Exeunt.*

---

[4]*Cried I aim?*] This is Douce's ingenious emendation for the Folio reading *Cride-game.* The earlier Quartos read *cried game.* "To cry aim," *i.e.* to stand beside the archer and to suggest the direction of his aim, is a technical phrase in archery. The host asks if he has not given the doctor good advice in his suit.

ACT III.

SCENE I. *A Field Near Frogmore.*

Enter SIR HUGH EVANS *and* SIMPLE

EVANS.   I pray you now, good Master Slender's serving-man, and
   friend Simple by your name, which way have you looked for
   Master Caius, that calls himself doctor of physic?
SIM.   Marry, sir, the pittie-ward,[1] the park-ward, every way; old
   Windsor way, and every way but the town way.
EVANS.   I most fehemently desire you you will also look that way.
SIM.   I will, sir.   [*Exit.*
EVANS.   Pless my soul, how full of chollors I am, and trempling of
   mind!—I shall be glad if he have deceived me.—How melan-
   cholies I am!—I will knog his urinals about his knave's costard
   when I have goot opportunities for the ork.—Pless my soul!—
                                                                      [*Sings.*

> To shallow rivers, to whose falls
> Melodious birds sings madrigals;
> There will we make our peds of roses,
> And a thousand fragrant posies.[2]
> To shallow—

Mercy on me! I have a great dispositions to cry.   [*Sings.*

---

[1]*pittie-ward*] This word, which is altered in the second and later Folios to *pitty-wary*, has
not been satisfactorily explained. The early emendation *city-ward* circumvents the dif-
ficulty. The suggestion that the word is equivalent to "pitwards," towards the pit, *i.e.* a
sawpit or gravel pit (in or about Windsor), is speciously supported by the mention of
"a sawpit," *infra*, IV, iv; of "a pit hard by Herne's oak," V, iii; and of "the pit," V, iv.
From the fact that medieval Bristol was credited by William of Worcester with a street
called "Via de Pyttey," and with a gate called "Pyttey Gate," it may be that a like name
was applied to some thoroughfare of Elizabethan Windsor.
[2]*To shallow rivers, etc.*] These four lines form part of the lyric "Come live with me and
be my love" (assigned to Christopher Marlowe), which was first printed in Jaggard's pi-
ratical miscellany called *"The Passionate Pilgrime*, By W. Shakespeare, 1599."

Melodious birds sing madrigals—
Whenas I sat in Pabylon[3]—
And a thousand vagram posies.
To shallow &c.

Re-enter SIMPLE

SIM.   Yonder he is coming, this way, Sir Hugh.
EVANS.   He's welcome.—

[*Sings.*

To shallow rivers, to whose falls—

Heaven prosper the right!—What weapons is he?
SIM.   No weapons, sir. There comes my master, Master Shallow, and another gentleman, from Frogmore, over the style, this way.
EVANS.   Pray you, give me my gown; or else keep it in your arms.

Enter PAGE, SHALLOW, *and* SLENDER

SHAL.   How now, master parson! Good morrow, good Sir Hugh. Keep a gamester from the dice, and a good student from his book, and it is wonderful.
SLEN. [*Aside*]   Ah, sweet Anne Page!
PAGE.   Save you, good Sir Hugh!
EVANS.   Pless you from his mercy sake, all of you!
SHAL.   What, the sword and the word! do you study them both, master parson?
PAGE.   And youthful still! in your doublet and hose this raw rheumatic day!
EVANS.   There is reasons and causes for it.
PAGE.   We are come to you to do a good office, master parson.
EVANS.   Fery well: what is it?
PAGE.   Yonder is a most reverend gentleman, who, belike having received wrong by some person, is at most odds with his own gravity and patience that ever you saw.
SHAL.   I have lived fourscore years and upward; I never heard a man of his place, gravity, and learning, so wide of his own respect.
EVANS.   What is he?
PAGE.   I think you know him; Master Doctor Caius, the renowned French physician.

---

[3]*Whenas I sat in Pabylon*] This is an interpolation into Marlowe's poem. Sir Hugh in his confusion jumbles his quotations. There is doubtless a reminiscence of *Ps.* cxxxvii, 1: "By the waters of Babylon we sat down and wept." But it should be noted that in the First (imperfect) Quarto of the play (1602) Evans prefixes to his repetition of Marlowe's lines the words (omitted in the Folio), "There dwelt a man in Babylon." That is the first line of another popular contemporary ballad known as *The Ballad of Constant Susanna.*

EVANS.   Got's will, and his passion of my heart! I had as lief you would
 tell me of a mess of porridge.

PAGE.   Why?

EVANS.   He has no more knowledge in Hibocrates and Galen,—and
 he is a knave besides; a cowardly knave as you would desires to be
 acquainted withal.

PAGE.   I warrant you, he's the man should fight with him.

SLEN. [*Aside*]   O sweet Anne Page!

SHAL.   It appears so, by his weapons. Keep them asunder: here comes
 Doctor Caius.

Enter HOST, CAIUS, *and* RUGBY

PAGE.   Nay, good master parson, keep in your weapon.

SHAL.   So do you, good master doctor.

HOST.   Disarm them, and let them question: let them keep their
 limbs whole, and hack our English.

CAIUS.   I pray you, let-a me speak a word with your ear. Verefore vill
 you not meet-a me?

EVANS. [*Aside to* CAIUS]   Pray you, use your patience: in good time.

CAIUS.   By gar, you are de coward, de Jack dog, John ape.

EVANS. [*Aside to* CAIUS]   Pray you, let us not be laughing-stocks to
 other men's humours; I desire you in friendship, and I will one
 way or other make you amends. [*Aloud*] I will knog your urinals
 about your knave's cogscomb for missing your meetings and
 appointments.

CAIUS.   Diable!—Jack Rugby,—mine host de Jarteer,—have I not stay
 for him to kill him? have I not, at de place I did appoint?

EVANS.   As I am a Christians soul, now, look you, this is the place appointed: I'll be judgement by mine host of the Garter.

HOST.   Peace, I say, Gallia and Gaul, French and Welsh, soul-curer
 and body-curer!

CAIUS.   Ay, dat is very good; excellent.

HOST.   Peace, I say! hear mine host of the Garter. Am I politic? am I
 subtle? am I a Machiavel? Shall I lose my doctor? no; he gives me
 the potions and the motions. Shall I lose my parson, my priest, my
 Sir Hugh? no; he gives me the proverbs and the no-verbs. Give me
 thy hand, terrestrial; so. Give me thy hand, celestial; so. Boys of
 art, I have deceived you both; I have directed you to wrong places:
 your hearts are mighty, your skins are whole, and let burnt sack be
 the issue. Come, lay their swords to pawn. Follow me, lads of
 peace; follow, follow, follow.

SHAL.   Trust me, a mad host. Follow, gentlemen, follow.

SLEN. [*Aside*]   O sweet Anne Page!

[*Exeunt* SHAL., SLEN., PAGE, *and* HOST.

CAIUS.   Ha, do I perceive dat? have you make-a de sot of us, ha, ha?

EVANS.   This is well; he has made us his vlouting-stog.[4]—I desire you
that we may be friends; and let us knog our prains together to be
revenge on this same scall,[5] scurvy, cogging companion, the host
of the Garter.

CAIUS.   By gar, with all my heart. He promise to bring me where is
Anne Page; by gar, he deceive me too.

EVANS.   Well, I will smite his noddles. Pray you, follow.   [*Exeunt.*

SCENE II. *The Street, in Windsor.*

Enter MISTRESS PAGE *and* ROBIN

MRS PAGE.   Nay, keep your way, little gallant; you were wont to be a
follower, but now you are a leader. Whether had you rather lead
mine eyes, or eye your master's heels?

ROB.   I had rather, forsooth, go before you like a man than follow him
like a dwarf.

MRS PAGE.   O, you are a flattering boy: now I see you'll be a courtier.

Enter FORD

FORD.   Well met, Mistress Page. Whither go you?

MRS PAGE.   Truly, sir, to see your wife. Is she at home?

FORD.   Ay; and as idle as she may hang together,[1] for want of company. I think, if your husbands were dead, you two would marry.

MRS PAGE.   Be sure of that,—two other husbands.

FORD.   Where had you this pretty weathercock?

MRS PAGE.   I cannot tell what the dickens his name is my husband
had him of.—What do you call your knight's name, sirrah?

ROB.   Sir John Falstaff.

FORD.   Sir John Falstaff!

MRS PAGE.   He, he; I can never hit on 's name. There is such a league
between my good man and he!—Is your wife at home indeed?

FORD.   Indeed she is.

MRS PAGE.   By your leave, sir: I am sick till I see her.
                                        [*Exeunt* MRS PAGE *and* ROBIN.

---

[4]*vlouting-stog*] Evans' mispronunciation of "flouting-stock," *i.e.* butt.
[5]*scall*] "Scall" is equivalent to "scald," and means much the same as "scurvy," the word
which follows.

---

[1]*as idle as she may hang together*] as idle as one can possibly be: a colloquialism equivalent to the modern slang "as idle as she can stick."

FORD.   Has Page any brains? hath he any eyes? hath he any thinking? Sure, they sleep; he hath no use of them. Why, this boy will carry a letter twenty mile, as easy as a cannon will shoot point-blank twelve score.[2] He pieces out his wife's inclination; he gives her folly motion and advantage: and now she's going to my wife, and Falstaff's boy with her. A man may hear this shower sing in the wind.[3] And Falstaff's boy with her! Good plots, they are laid; and our revolted wives share damnation together. Well; I will take him, then torture my wife, pluck the borrowed veil of modesty from the so seeming Mistress Page, divulge Page himself for a secure and wilful Actæon; and to these violent proceedings all my neighbours shall cry aim.[4] [*Clock heard.*] The clock gives me my cue, and my assurance bids me search: there I shall find Falstaff: I shall be rather praised for this than mocked; for it is as positive as the earth is firm that Falstaff is there: I will go.

Enter PAGE, SHALLOW, SLENDER, HOST, SIR HUGH EVANS, CAIUS, *and* RUGBY

SHAL., PAGE, &c.   Well met, Master Ford.

FORD.   Trust me, a good knot:[5] I have good cheer at home; and I pray you all go with me.

SHAL.   I must excuse myself, Master Ford.

SLEN.   And so must I, sir: we have appointed to dine with Mistress Anne, and I would not break with her for more money than I'll speak of.

SHAL.   We have lingered about a match between Anne Page and my cousin Slender, and this day we shall have our answer.

SLEN.   I hope I have your good will, father Page.

PAGE.   You have, Master Slender; I stand wholly for you:—but my wife, master doctor, is for you altogether.

CAIUS.   Ay, be-gar; and de maid is love-a me: my nursh-a Quickly tell me so mush.

HOST.   What say you to young Master Fenton? he capers, he dances, he has eyes of youth, he writes verses, he speaks holiday,[6] he smells April and May: he will carry 't, he will carry 't; 't is in his buttons;[7] he will carry 't.

---

[2]*twelve score*] twelve score yards.
[3]*may hear this shower . . . wind*] A phrase implying the coming of a storm, which is often heralded by a whistling or singing note in the rising wind.
[4]*cry aim*] give encouragement.
[5]*a good knot*] a welcome gathering of friends.
[6]*speaks holiday*] uses choice phrases.
[7]*in his buttons*] altogether in his compass or ability.

PAGE.   Not by my consent, I promise you. The gentleman is of no hav-ing:[8] he kept company with the wild prince and Poins;[9] he is of too high a region;[10] he knows too much. No, he shall not knit a knot in his fortunes with the finger of my substance: if he take her, let him take her simply; the wealth I have waits on my consent, and my consent goes not that way.

FORD.   I beseech you heartily, some of you go home with me to din-ner: besides your cheer, you shall have sport; I will show you a monster. Master doctor, you shall go; so shall you, Master Page; and you, Sir Hugh.

SHAL.   Well, fare you well: we shall have the freer wooing at Master Page's.   [*Exeunt* SHAL. *and* SLEN.

CAIUS.   Go home, John Rugby; I come anon.   [*Exit* RUGBY.

HOST.   Farewell, my hearts: I will to my honest knight Falstaff, and drink canary with him.   [*Exit.*

FORD. [*Aside*]   I think I shall drink in pipe-wine[11] first with him; I'll make him dance. Will you go, gentles?

ALL.   Have with you to see this monster.   [*Exeunt.*

SCENE III. *A Room in Ford's House.*

Enter MISTRESS FORD *and* MISTRESS PAGE

MRS FORD.   What, John! What, Robert!

MRS PAGE.   Quickly, quickly!—is the buck-basket[1]—

MRS FORD.   I warrant. What, Robin, I say!

Enter Servants *with a basket*

MRS PAGE.   Come, come, come.

MRS FORD.   Here, set it down.

MRS PAGE.   Give your men the charge; we must be brief.

---

[8]*no having*] no property or fortune.

[9]*the wild prince and Poins*] Prince Hal, afterwards Henry V, and his favourite com-panion Poins, both of whom are leading characters in the two parts of *Hen. IV.*

[10]*too high a region*] too high a rank, too highly placed. "Region" is often applied to the highest layers of the atmospheric air.

[11]*drink in pipe-wine*] There is a pun on the word "pipe," which is employed in the dou-ble sense of an instrument used for dance-music and a liquid-measure. Similarly, "ca-nary" is both a dance and a wine. The meaning is to the same effect as that of the next sentence: "I'll make him dance." "Drink in" is equivalent to "drink." "Pipe-wine" is literally wine drawn from the pipe (or barrel of two hogsheads).

---

[1]*buck-basket*] The basket in which dirty clothes were sent to be "bucked," or washed by the thorough process commonly known as "bucking."

MRS FORD.   Marry, as I told you before, John and Robert, be ready here hard by in the brew-house; and when I suddenly call you, come forth, and, without any pause or staggering, take this basket on your shoulders: that done, trudge with it in all haste, and carry it among the whitsters in Datchet-mead, and there empty it in the muddy ditch close by the Thames side.

MRS PAGE.   You will do it?

MRS FORD.   I ha' told them over and over; they lack no direction. Be gone, and come when you are called.   [*Exeunt* Servants.

MRS PAGE.   Here comes little Robin.

Enter ROBIN

MRS FORD.   How now, my eyas-musket! what news with you?

ROB.   My master, Sir John, is come in at your backdoor, Mistress Ford, and requests your company.

MRS PAGE.   You little Jack-a-Lent,[2] have you been true to us?

ROB.   Ay, I'll be sworn. My master knows not of your being here, and hath threatened to put me into everlasting liberty, if I tell you of it; for he swears he'll turn me away.

MRS PAGE.   Thou 'rt a good boy: this secrecy of thine shall be a tailor to thee, and shall make thee a new doublet and hose. I'll go hide me.

MRS FORD.   Do so. Go tell thy master I am alone. [*Exit* ROBIN.] Mistress Page, remember you your cue.

MRS PAGE.   I warrant thee; if I do not act it, hiss me.   [*Exit.*

MRS FORD.   Go to, then: we'll use this unwholesome humidity, this gross watery pumpion; we'll teach him to know turtles from jays.[3]

Enter FALSTAFF

FAL.   "Have I caught" thee, "my heavenly jewel?"[4] Why, now let me die, for I have lived long enough: this is the period of my ambition: O this blessed hour!

MRS FORD.   O sweet Sir John!

FAL.   Mistress Ford, I cannot cog, I cannot prate, Mistress Ford. Now shall I sin in my wish: I would thy husband were dead: I'll speak it before the best lord; I would make thee my lady.

MRS FORD.   I your lady, Sir John! alas, I should be a pitiful lady!

[2]*Jack-a-Lent*] a puppet, at which, during Lent, children at play flung sticks or stones.
[3]*turtles from jays*] faithful wives from loose women. In Italian *putta* means both jay and harlot.
[4]*"Have I caught" . . . "my heavenly jewel?"*] These words form the first line of the second song in Sir Philip Sidney's *Astrophel and Stella* (first published in 1591). The early Quartos of the play rightly omit *thee*.

FAL.   Let the court of France show me such another. I see how thine eye would emulate the diamond: thou hast the right arched beauty of the brow that becomes the ship-tire, the tire-valiant, or any tire of Venetian admittance.[5]

MRS FORD.   A plain kerchief, Sir John: my brows become nothing else; nor that well neither.

FAL.   By the Lord, thou art a traitor to say so: thou wouldst make an absolute courtier; and the firm fixture of thy foot would give an excellent motion to thy gait in a semi-circled farthingale. I see what thou wert, if Fortune thy foe[6] were not, Nature thy friend. Come, thou canst not hide it.

MRS FORD.   Believe me, there's no such thing in me.

FAL.   What made me love thee? let that persuade thee there's something extraordinary in thee. Come, I cannot cog, and say thou art this and that, like a many of these lisping hawthorn-buds, that come like women in men's apparel, and smell like Bucklersbury[7] in simple time; I cannot: but I love thee; none but thee; and thou deservest it.

MRS FORD.   Do not betray me, sir. I fear you love Mistress Page.

FAL.   Thou mightst as well say I love to walk by the Counter-gate,[8] which is as hateful to me as the reek of a lime-kiln.

MRS FORD.   Well, heaven knows how I love you; and you shall one day find it.

FAL.   Keep in that mind; I'll deserve it.

MRS FORD.   Nay, I must tell you, so you do; or else I could not be in that mind.

ROB. [*Within*]   Mistress Ford, Mistress Ford! here's Mistress Page at the door, sweating, and blowing, and looking wildly, and would needs speak with you presently.

---

[5]*the ship-tire . . . of Venetian admittance*] Falstaff refers to three kinds of headdress, firstly that shaped like a ship, secondly "the tire-valiant," and lastly that of the quality held in esteem at Venice, in the Venetian fashion. The "tire-valiant" is not easy to explain. The early Quartos read "tire-vellet" (*i.e.* velvet), which makes good sense. Stubbes in his *Anatomie of Abuses*, denounces with heat velvet ornaments for the head. "Tire-valiant" can only mean headdress of very "brave" *i.e.* showy, design.

[6]*Fortune thy foe*] "Fortune my foe" are the opening words of a popular ballad deploring the caprices of Fortune. It is found in early ballad collections, and runs to twenty-two stanzas. The opening line runs, "*Fortune my foe,* why dost thou frown on me?"

[7]*Bucklersbury*] A street at the east end of Cheapside, London, which was full of apothecaries' shops and was redolent of medicinal herbs or simples in early summer, when they were freshly stored.

[8]*Counter-gate*] the gate of the gaol. Two prisons in the city of London were known respectively as the Wood Street *Counter*, the Poultry *Counter*. "The *Counter*" was the title of the gaol in Southwark.

FAL.   She shall not see me: I will ensconce me behind the arras.[9]
MRS FORD.   Pray you, do so: she's a very tattling woman.

[FALSTAFF *hides himself.*

Re-enter MISTRESS PAGE *and* ROBIN

What's the matter? how now!
MRS PAGE.   O Mistress Ford, what have you done? You're shamed, you're overthrown, you're undone for ever!
MRS FORD.   What's the matter, good Mistress Page?
MRS PAGE.   O well-a-day, Mistress Ford! having an honest man to your husband, to give him such cause of suspicion!
MRS FORD.   What cause of suspicion?
MRS PAGE.   What cause of suspicion! Out upon you! how am I mistook in you!
MRS FORD.   Why, alas, what's the matter?
MRS PAGE.   Your husband's coming hither, woman, with all the officers in Windsor, to search for a gentleman that he says is here now in the house, by your consent, to take an ill advantage of his absence: you are undone.
MRS FORD.   'T is not so, I hope.
MRS PAGE.   Pray heaven it be not so, that you have such a man here! but 't is most certain your husband's coming, with half Windsor at his heels, to search for such a one. I come before to tell you. If you know yourself clear, why, I am glad of it; but if you have a friend here, convey, convey him out. Be not amazed; call all your senses to you; defend your reputation, or bid farewell to your good life for ever.
MRS FORD.   What shall I do? There is a gentleman my dear friend; and I fear not mine own shame so much as his peril: I had rather than a thousand pound he were out of the house.
MRS PAGE.   For shame! never stand "you had rather" and "you had rather:" your husband's here at hand; bethink you of some conveyance: in the house you cannot hide him. O, how have you deceived me! Look, here is a basket: if he be of any reasonable stature, he may creep in here; and throw foul linen upon him, as if it were going to bucking: or,—it is whiting-time,[10]—send him by your two men to Datchet-mead.
MRS FORD.   He's too big to go in there. What shall I do?
FAL. [*Coming forward*]   Let me see 't, let me see 't, O, let me see 't!— I'll in, I'll in.—Follow your friend's counsel.—I'll in.

---

[9]*the arras*] the tapestry which hung from wooden rods at a little distance from the wall of the room.
[10]*whiting-time*] bleaching-time, spring-time.

MRS PAGE.   What, Sir John Falstaff! Are these your letters, knight?

FAL.   I love thee.[11]—Help me away.—Let me creep in here.—I'll never—   [*Gets into the basket; they cover him with foul linen.*

MRS PAGE.   Help to cover your master, boy.—Call your men, Mistress Ford.—You dissembling knight!

MRS FORD.   What, John! Robert! John!   [*Exit* ROBIN.

Re-enter Servants

Go take up these clothes here quickly.—Where's the cowl-staff? look, how you drumble!—Carry them to the laundress in Datchet-mead; quickly, come.

Enter FORD, PAGE, CAIUS, *and* SIR HUGH EVANS

FORD.   Pray you, come near: if I suspect without cause, why then make sport at me; then let me be your jest; I deserve it.—How now! whither bear you this?

SERV.   To the laundress, forsooth.

MRS FORD.   Why, what have you to do whither they bear it? You were best meddle with buck-washing.

FORD.   Buck!—I would I could wash myself of the buck!—Buck, buck, buck! Ay, buck; I warrant you, buck; and of the season too, it shall appear. [*Exeunt* Servants *with the basket.*] Gentlemen, I have dreamed to-night; I'll tell you my dream. Here, here, here be my keys: ascend my chambers; search, seek, find out: I'll warrant we'll unkennel the fox. Let me stop this way first. [*Locking the door.*] So, now uncape.[12]

PAGE.   Good Master Ford, be contented: you wrong yourself too much.

FORD.   True, Master Page. Up, gentlemen; you shall see sport anon: follow me, gentlemen.   [*Exit.*

EVANS.   This is fery fantastical humours and jealousies.

CAIUS.   By gar, 't is no the fashion of France; it is not jealous in France.

PAGE.   Nay, follow him, gentlemen; see the issue of his search.
   [*Exeunt* PAGE, CAIUS, *and* EVANS.

MRS PAGE.   Is there not a double excellency in this?

MRS FORD.   I know not which pleases me better, that my husband is deceived, or Sir John.

---

[11]*I love thee*] Malone and most of his successors add from the early Quartos, *and none but thee.* The words sound like a quotation from some old song. Falstaff had already told Mrs. Ford "I love thee; none but thee."

[12]*uncape*] No other example of this word is found. The meaning is obviously "uncouple" (of hounds in hunting). "Cape" was occasionally used in the sense of "collar."

MRS PAGE.   What a taking was he in when your husband asked who was in the basket!

MRS FORD.   I am half afraid he will have need of washing; so throwing him into the water will do him a benefit.

MRS PAGE.   Hang him, dishonest rascal! I would all of the same strain were in the same distress.

MRS FORD.   I think my husband hath some special suspicion of Falstaff's being here; for I never saw him so gross in his jealousy till now.

MRS PAGE.   I will lay a plot to try that; and we will yet have more tricks with Falstaff: his dissolute disease will scarce obey this medicine.

MRS FORD.   Shall we send that foolish carrion,[13] Mistress Quickly, to him, and excuse his throwing into the water; and give him another hope, to betray him to another punishment?

MRS PAGE.   We will do it: let him be sent for tomorrow, eight o'clock, to have amends.

Re-enter FORD, PAGE, CAIUS, *and* SIR HUGH EVANS

FORD.   I cannot find him: may be the knave bragged of that he could not compass.

MRS PAGE. [*Aside to* MRS FORD]   Heard you that?

MRS FORD.   You use me well,[14] Master Ford, do you?

FORD.   Ay, I do so.

MRS FORD.   Heaven make you better than your thoughts!

FORD.   Amen!

MRS PAGE.   You do yourself mighty wrong, Master Ford.

FORD.   Ay, ay; I must bear it.

EVANS.   If there be any pody in the house, and in the chambers, and in the coffers, and in the presses, heaven forgive my sins at the day of judgement!

CAIUS.   By gar, nor I too: there is no bodies.

PAGE.   Fie, fie, Master Ford! are you not ashamed? What spirit, what devil suggests this imagination? I would not ha' your distemper in this kind for the wealth of Windsor Castle.

FORD.   'T is my fault, Master Page: I suffer for it.

EVANS.   You suffer for a pad conscience: your wife is as honest a 'omans as I will desires among five thousand, and five hundred too.

CAIUS.   By gar, I see 't is an honest woman.

FORD.   Well, I promised you a dinner.—Come, come, walk in the Park: I pray you, pardon me; I will hereafter make known to you

[13]*carrion*] a term of contempt.
[14]*You use me well*] Theobald prefixed the words *Ay, ay; peace:* from the early Quartos.

why I have done this.—Come, wife; come, Mistress Page.—I pray
you, pardon me; pray heartily pardon me.

PAGE.   Let's go in, gentlemen; but, trust me, we'll mock him. I do in-
vite you to-morrow morning to my house to breakfast: after, we'll
a-birding together; I have a fine hawk for the bush. Shall it be so?

FORD.   Any thing.

EVANS.   If there is one, I shall make two in the company.

CAIUS.   If there be one or two, I shall make-a the turd.

FORD.   Pray you, go, Master Page.

EVANS.   I pray you now, remembrance to-morrow on the lousy knave,
mine host.

CAIUS.   Dat is good; by gar, with all my heart!

EVANS.   A lousy knave, to have his gibes and his mockeries!

[*Exeunt.*

SCENE IV. *A Room in Page's House.*

Enter FENTON *and* ANNE PAGE

FENT.   I see I cannot get thy father's love;
Therefore no more turn me to him, sweet Nan.

ANNE.   Alas, how then?

FENT.   Why, thou must be thyself.
He doth object I am too great of birth;
And that, my state being gall'd with my expense,
I seek to heal it only by his wealth:
Besides these, other bars he lays before me,—
My riots past, my wild societies;[1]
And tells me 't is a thing impossible
I should love thee but as a property.

ANNE.   May be he tells you true.

FENT.   No, heaven so speed me in my time to come!
Albeit I will confess thy father's wealth
Was the first motive that I woo'd thee, Anne:
Yet, wooing thee, I found thee of more value
Than stamps in gold[2] or sums in sealed bags;
And 't is the very riches of thyself
That now I aim at.

ANNE.   Gentle Master Fenton,
Yet seek my father's love; still seek it, sir:

---

[1]*societies*] associates, companions.
[2]*stamps in gold*] coins.

If opportunity and humblest suit
Cannot attain it, why, then,—hark you hither!

[*They converse apart.*

Enter SHALLOW, SLENDER, *and* MISTRESS QUICKLY

SHAL.   Break their talk, Mistress Quickly: my kinsman shall speak for
himself.

SLEN.   I'll make a shaft or a bolt[3] on 't: 'slid, 't is but venturing.

SHAL.   Be not dismayed.

SLEN.   No, she shall not dismay me: I care not for that, but that I am
afeard.

QUICK.   Hark ye; Master Slender would speak a word with you.

ANNE.   I come to him. [*Aside*] This is my father's choice.
O, what a world of vile ill-favour'd faults
Looks handsome in three hundred pounds a-year!

QUICK.   And how does good Master Fenton? Pray you, a word with
you.

SHAL.   She's coming; to her, coz. O boy, thou hadst a father!

SLEN.   I had a father, Mistress Anne; my uncle can tell you good jests
of him. Pray you, uncle, tell Mistress Anne the jest, how my father
stole two geese out of a pen, good uncle.

SHAL.   Mistress Anne, my cousin loves you.

SLEN.   Ay, that I do; as well as I love any woman in Gloucestershire.

SHAL.   He will maintain you like a gentlewoman.

SLEN.   Ay, that I will, come cut and long-tail,[4] under the degree of a
squire.

SHAL.   He will make you a hundred and fifty pounds ointure.

ANNE.   Good Master Shallow, let him woo for himself.

SHAL.   Marry, I thank you for it; I thank you for that good comfort. She
calls you, coz: I'll leave you.

ANNE.   Now, Master Slender,—

SLEN.   Now, good Mistress Anne,—

ANNE.   What is your will?

SLEN.   My will! od's heartlings, that's a pretty jest indeed! I ne'er made
my will yet, I thank heaven; I am not such a sickly creature, I give
heaven praise.

ANNE.   I mean, Master Slender, what would you with me?

SLEN.   Truly, for mine own part, I would little or nothing with you.
Your father and my uncle hath made motions: if it be my luck, so;

[3]*shaft or a bolt*] proverbial expression for "I'll do it one way or another." A shaft was a
long, slender arrow; a bolt, a short, thick one.
[4]*come cut and long-tail*] whatever come, alluding to dogs with short and long tails;
equivalent to "bob-tag and rag-tail."

if not, happy man be his dole![5] They can tell you how things go
better that I can: you may ask your father; here he comes.

Enter PAGE *and* MISTRESS PAGE

PAGE.   Now, Master Slender: love him, daughter Anne.—
    Why, how now! what does Master Fenton here?
    You wrong me, sir, thus still to haunt my house:
    I told you, sir, my daughter is disposed of.
FENT.   Nay, Master Page, be not impatient.
MRS PAGE.   Good Master Fenton, come not to my child.
PAGE.   She is no match for you.
FENT.   Sir, will you hear me?
PAGE.   No, good Master Fenton.
    Come, Master Shallow; come, son Slender, in.
    Knowing my mind, you wrong me, Master Fenton.
                  [Exeunt PAGE, SHAL., *and* SLEN.
QUICK.   Speak to Mistress Page.
FENT.   Good Mistress Page, for that I love your daughter
    In such a righteous fashion as I do,
    Perforce, against all checks, rebukes and manners,
    I must advance the colours of my love,
    And not retire: let me have your good will.
ANNE.   Good mother, do not marry me to yond fool.
MRS PAGE.   I mean it not; I seek you a better husband.
QUICK.   That's my master, master doctor.
ANNE.   Alas, I had rather be set quick i' the earth,
    And bowl'd to death with turnips!
MRS PAGE.   Come, trouble not yourself. Good Master Fenton,
    I will not be your friend nor enemy:
    My daughter will I question how she loves you,
    And as I find her, so am I affected.
    Till then farewell, sir: she must needs go in;
    Her father will be angry.
FENT.   Farewell, gentle mistress: farewell, Nan.
                  [Exeunt MRS PAGE *and* ANNE.
QUICK.   This is my doing now: "Nay," said I, "will you cast away your
    child on a fool, and a physician?[6] Look on Master Fenton:" this is
    my doing.

---

[5]*happy man be his dole*] good fortune go with you.
[6]*a fool, and a physician*] The two words were constantly brought together colloquially,
    apparently in vague allusion to the proverbial phrase, "A man of forty is either a fool
    or his own physician." Some editors read *or* for *and*.

FENT.   I thank thee; and I pray thee, once to-night
    Give my sweet Nan this ring: there's for thy pains.

QUICK.   Now heaven send thee good fortune! [*Exit* FENTON.] A kind
    heart he hath: a woman would run through fire and water for such
    a kind heart. But yet I would my master had Mistress Anne; or I
    would Master Slender had her; or, in sooth, I would Master
    Fenton had her: I will do what I can for them all three; for so I
    have promised, and I'll be as good as my word; but speciously[7] for
    Master Fenton. Well, I must of another errand to Sir John Falstaff
    from my two mistresses: what a beast am I to slack it!   [*Exit.*

SCENE V. *A Room in the Garter Inn.*

Enter FALSTAFF *and* BARDOLPH

FAL.   Bardolph, I say,—

BARD.   Here, sir.

FAL.   Go fetch me a quart of sack; put a toast in 't. [*Exit* BARD.] Have
    I lived to be carried in a basket, like a barrow of butcher's offal,
    and to be thrown in the Thames? Well, if I be served such another
    trick, I'll have my brains ta'en out, and buttered, and give them to
    a dog for a new-year's gift. The rogues slighted me into the river
    with as little remorse as they would have drowned a blind bitch's
    puppies,[1] fifteen i' the litter: and you may know by my size that I
    have a kind of alacrity in sinking; if the bottom were as deep as
    hell, I should down. I had been drowned, but that the shore was
    shelvy and shallow,—a death that I abhor; for the water swells a
    man; and what a thing should I have been when I had been
    swelled! I should have been a mountain of mummy.

Re-enter BARDOLPH *with sack*

BARD.   Here's Mistress Quickly, sir, to speak with you.

FAL.   Come, let me pour in some sack to the Thames water; for my
    belly's as cold as if I had swallowed snowballs for pills to cool the
    reins. Call her in.

BARD.   Come in, woman!

Enter MISTRESS QUICKLY

QUICK.   By your leave; I cry you mercy: give your worship good
    morrow.

---

[7]*speciously*] blunder for "especially."

[1]*blind bitch's puppies*] a colloquial inversion for a "bitch's blind puppies."

FAL. Take away these chalices. Go brew me a pottle of sack finely.

BARD. With eggs, sir?

FAL. Simple of itself; I'll no pullet-sperm in my brewage. [*Exit* BARDOLPH.] How now!

QUICK. Marry, sir, I come to your worship from Mistress Ford.

FAL. Mistress Ford! I have had ford enough; I was thrown into the ford; I have my belly full of ford.

QUICK. Alas the day! good heart, that was not her fault: she does so take on with[2] her men; they mistook their erection.[3]

FAL. So did I mine, to build upon a foolish woman's promise.

QUICK. Well, she laments, sir, for it, that it would yearn your heart to see it. Her husband goes this morning a-birding; she desires you once more to come to her between eight and nine: I must carry her word quickly: she'll make you amends, I warrant you.

FAL. Well, I will visit her: tell her so; and bid her think what a man is: let her consider his frailty, and then judge of my merit.

QUICK. I will tell her.

FAL. Do so. Between nine and ten, sayest thou?

QUICK. Eight and nine, sir.

FAL. Well, be gone: I will not miss her.

QUICK. Peace be with you, sir. [*Exit.*

FAL. I marvel I hear not of Master Brook; he sent me word to stay within: I like his money well.—O, here he comes.

Enter FORD

FORD. Bless you, sir!

FAL. Now, Master Brook,—you come to know what hath passed between me and Ford's wife?

FORD. That, indeed, Sir John, is my business.

FAL. Master Brook, I will not lie to you: I was at her house the hour she appointed me.

FORD. And sped you, sir?

FAL. Very ill-favouredly, Master Brook.

FORD. How so, sir? Did she change her determination?

FAL. No, Master Brook; but the peaking Cornuto her husband, Master Brook, dwelling in a continual 'larum of jealousy, comes me in the instant of our encounter, after we had embraced, kissed, protested, and, as it were, spoke the prologue of our comedy; and at his heels a rabble of his companions, thither provoked and instigated by his distemper, and, forsooth, to search his house for his wife's love.

---

[2]*take on with*] rage at, get in a passion with.
[3]*erection*] blunder for "direction."

FORD.   What, while you were there?

FAL.   While I was there.

FORD.   And did he search for you, and could not find you?

FAL.   You shall hear. As good luck would have it, comes in one Mistress Page; gives intelligence of Ford's approach; and, in her invention and Ford's wife's distraction, they conveyed me into a buck-basket.

FORD.   A buck-basket!

FAL.   By the Lord, a buck-basket!—rammed me in with foul shirts and smocks, socks, foul stockings, greasy napkins; that, Master Brook, there was the rankest compound of villanous smell that ever offended nostril.

FORD.   And how long lay you there?

FAL.   Nay, you shall hear, Master Brook, what I have suffered to bring this woman to evil for your good. Being thus crammed in the basket, a couple of Ford's knaves, his hinds, were called forth by their mistress to carry me in the name of foul clothes to Datchet-lane: they took me on their shoulders; met the jealous knave their master in the door, who asked them once or twice what they had in their basket: I quaked for fear, lest the lunatic knave would have searched it; but fate, ordaining he should be a cuckold, held his hand. Well: on went he for a search, and away went I for foul clothes. But mark the sequel, Master Brook: I suffered the pangs of three several deaths; first, an intolerable fright, to be detected with[4] a jealous rotten bell-wether; next, to be compassed, like a good bilbo,[5] in the circumference of a peck, hilt to point, heel to head, and then, to be stopped in, like a strong distillation, with stinking clothes that fretted in their own grease: think of that,—a man of my kidney,—think of that,—that am as subject to heat as butter; a man of continual dissolution and thaw: it was a miracle to 'scape suffocation. And in the height of this bath, when I was more than half stewed in grease, like a Dutch dish, to be thrown into the Thames, and cooled, glowing hot, in that surge, like a horse-shoe; think of that,—hissing hot,—think of that, Master Brook.

FORD.   In good sadness,[6] sir, I am sorry that for my sake you have suffered all this. My suit, then, is desperate; you'll undertake her no more?

FAL.   Master Brook, I will be thrown into Etna, as I have been into

---

[4]*detected with*] detected by.

[5]*bilbo*] the blade of a bilbo, *i.e.* a Spanish sword from Bilbao, which was extremely flexible and elastic.

[6]*In good sadness*] In sober earnest.

Thames, ere I will leave her thus. Her husband is this morning
gone a-birding: I have received from her another embassy of meeting; 'twixt eight and nine is the hour, Master Brook.

FORD.   'T is past eight already, sir.

FAL.   Is it? I will then address me to my appointment. Come to me at
your convenient leisure, and you shall know how I speed; and the
conclusion shall be crowned with your enjoying her. Adieu. You
shall have her, Master Brook; Master Brook, you shall cuckold
Ford.   [*Exit.*

FORD.   Hum! ha! is this a vision? is this a dream? do I sleep? Master
Ford, awake! awake, Master Ford! there's a hole made in your best
coat, Master Ford. This 't is to be married! this 't is to have linen
and buck-baskets! Well, I will proclaim myself what I am: I will
now take the lecher; he is at my house; he cannot 'scape me; 't is
impossible he should; he cannot creep into a halfpenny purse,[7]
nor into a pepper-box: but, lest the devil that guides him should
aid him, I will search impossible places. Though what I am I cannot avoid, yet to be what I would not shall not make me tame: if I
have horns to make one mad, let the proverb go with me, — I'll be
horn-mad.   [*Exit.*

----

[7]*halfpenny purse*] The halfpenny, which was of silver, was a very small coin.

ACT IV.

SCENE I. A Street.

Enter MISTRESS PAGE, MISTRESS QUICKLY, *and* WILLIAM

MRS PAGE.   Is he at Master Ford's already, think'st thou?

QUICK.   Sure he is by this, or will be presently: but, truly, he is very courageous[1] mad about his throwing into the water. Mistress Ford desires you to come suddenly.

MRS PAGE.   I'll be with her by and by; I'll but bring my young man here to school. Look, where his master comes; 't is a playing-day, I see.

Enter SIR HUGH EVANS

How now, Sir Hugh! no school to-day?

EVANS.   No; Master Slender is let the boys leave to play.

QUICK.   Blessing of his heart!

MRS PAGE.   Sir Hugh, my husband says my son profits nothing in the world at his book. I pray you, ask him some questions in his accidence.

EVANS.   Come hither, William; hold up your head; come.

MRS PAGE.   Come on, sirrah; hold up your head; answer your master, be not afraid.

EVANS.   William, how many numbers is in nouns?

WILL.   Two.

QUICK.   Truly, I thought there had been one number more, because they say, "Od's nouns."

EVANS.   Peace your tattlings! What is "fair," William?

WILL.   Pulcher.

QUICK.   Polecats! there are fairer things than polecats, sure.

EVANS.   You are a very simplicity 'oman: I pray you, peace.—What is "lapis," William?

---

[1]*courageous*] apparently a blunder for "outrageous."

49

WILL.   A stone.
EVANS.   And what is "a stone," William?
WILL.   A pebble.
EVANS.   No, it is "lapis": I pray you, remember in your prain.
WILL.   Lapis.
EVANS.   That is a good William. What is he, William, that does lend articles?
WILL.   Articles are borrowed of the pronoun, and be thus declined, "Singulariter, nominativo, hic, hæc, hoc.
EVANS.   Nominativo, hig, hag, hog; pray you, mark: genitivo, hujus. Well, what is your accusative case?
WILL.   Accusativo, hinc.
EVANS.   I pray you, have your remembrance, child; accusativo, hung, hang, hog.
QUICK.   "Hang-hog" is Latin for bacon, I warrant you.
EVANS.   Leave your prabbles,[2] 'oman.—What is the focative case, William?
WILL.   O,—vocativo, O.
EVANS.   Remember, William; focative is caret.
QUICK.   And that's a good root.
EVANS.   'Oman, forbear.
MRS PAGE.   Peace!
EVANS.   What is your genitive case plural, William?
WILL.   Genitive case!
EVANS.   Ay.
WILL.   Genitive,—horum, harum, horum.
QUICK.   Vengeance of Jenny's case! fie on her! never name her, child, if she be a whore.
EVANS.   For shame, 'oman.
QUICK.   You do ill to teach the child such words:—he teaches him to hick and to hack,[3] which they'll do fast enough of themselves, and to call "horum":—fie upon you!
EVANS.   'Oman, art thou lunatics? hast thou no understandings for thy cases, and the numbers of the genders? Thou art as foolish Christian creatures as I would desires.
MRS PAGE.   Prithee, hold thy peace.
EVANS.   Show me now, William, some declensions of your pronouns.
WILL.   Forsooth, I have forgot.
EVANS.   It is qui, quæ, quod: if you forget your "quies," your "quæs,"

---

[2]*prabbles*] chatter.
[3]*hick and to hack*] apparently used in a somewhat ribald significance.

and your "quods," you must be preeches.[4] Go your ways, and play;
    go.

MRS PAGE.   He is a better scholar than I thought he was.

EVANS.   He is a good sprag memory. Farewell, Mistress Page.

MRS PAGE.   Adieu, good Sir Hugh.   [*Exit* SIR HUGH.
    Get you home, boy. Come, we stay too long.   [*Exeunt.*

SCENE II. *A Room in Ford's House.*

Enter FALSTAFF *and* MISTRESS FORD

FAL.   Mistress Ford, your sorrow hath eaten up my sufferance. I see
    you are obsequious in your love,[1] and I profess requital to a hair's
    breadth; not only, Mistress Ford, in the simple office of love, but
    in all the accoutrement, complement, and ceremony of it. But are
    you sure of your husband now?

MRS FORD.   He's a-birding, sweet Sir John.

MRS PAGE. [*Within*]   What, ho, gossip Ford! what, ho!

MRS FORD.   Step into the chamber, Sir John.   [*Exit* FALSTAFF.

Enter MISTRESS PAGE

MRS PAGE.   How now, sweetheart! who's at home besides yourself?

MRS FORD.   Why, none but mine own people.

MRS PAGE.   Indeed!

MRS FORD.   No, certainly. [*Aside to her*] Speak louder.

MRS PAGE.   Truly, I am so glad you have nobody here.

MRS FORD.   Why?

MRS PAGE.   Why, woman, your husband is in his old lunes[2] again: he
    so takes on yonder with[3] my husband; so rails against all married
    mankind; so curses all Eve's daughters, of what complexion so-
    ever; and so buffets himself on the forehead, crying, "Peer out,
    peer out!"[4] that any madness I ever yet beheld seemed but tame-
    ness, civility, and patience, to this his distemper he is in now: I am
    glad the fat knight is not here.

MRS FORD.   Why, does he talk of him?

---

[4]*preeches*] breeches: breeched, *i.e.* flogged.

[1]*your sorrow . . . love*] your grief has blotted out the memory of my sufferings. I see your
  devotion (to me) is seriously meant (of the seriousness attaching to funereal rites or
  obsequies).

[2]*lunes*] "Lunes" means "fits of lunacy."

[3]*takes on . . . with*] gets in a passion with.

[4]*Peer out, peer out!*] Horns, make your appearance, come forth!

MRS PAGE.   Of none but him; and swears he was carried out, the last time he searched for him, in a basket; protests to my husband he is now here; and hath drawn him and the rest of their company from their sport, to make another experiment of his suspicion: but I am glad the knight is not here; now he shall see his own foolery.

MRS FORD.   How near is he, Mistress Page?

MRS PAGE.   Hard by, at street end; he will be here anon.

MRS FORD.   I am undone!—the knight is here.

MRS PAGE.   Why, then, you are utterly shamed, and he's but a dead man. What a woman are you!—Away with him, away with him! better shame than murder.

MRS FORD.   Which way should he go? how should I bestow him? Shall I put him into the basket again?

Re-enter FALSTAFF

FAL.   No, I'll come no more i' the basket. May I not go out ere he come?

MRS PAGE.   Alas, three of Master Ford's brothers watch the door with pistols, that none shall issue out; otherwise you might slip away ere he came. But what make you here?

FAL.   What shall I do?—I'll creep up into the chimney.

MRS FORD.   There they always use to discharge their birding-pieces. Creep into the kiln-hole.

FAL.   Where is it?

MRS FORD.   He will seek there, on my word. Neither press, coffer, chest, trunk, well, vault, but he hath an abstract[5] for the remembrance of such places, and goes to them by his note: there is no hiding you in the house.

FAL.   I'll go out, then.

MRS PAGE.   If you go out in your own semblance, you die, Sir John. Unless you go out disguised,—

MRS FORD.   How might we disguise him?

MRS PAGE.   Alas the day, I know not! There is no woman's gown big enough for him; otherwise he might put on a hat, a muffler, and a kerchief, and so escape.

FAL.   Good hearts, devise something: any extremity rather than a mischief.

MRS FORD.   My maid's aunt, the fat woman of Brentford, has a gown above.

MRS PAGE.   On my word, it will serve him; she's as big as he is: and there's her thrummed hat,[6] and her muffler too. Run up, Sir John.

[5]*abstract*] short list or inventory.
[6]*thrummed hat*] hat made of coarse yarn.

MRS FORD.   Go, go, sweet Sir John: Mistress Page and I will look some linen for your head.

MRS PAGE.   Quick, quick! we'll come dress you straight: put on the gown the while.   [Exit FALSTAFF.

MRS FORD.   I would my husband would meet him in this shape: he cannot abide the old woman of Brentford; he swears she's a witch; forbade her my house, and hath threatened to beat her.

MRS PAGE.   Heaven guide him to thy husband's cudgel, and the devil guide his cudgel afterwards!

MRS FORD.   But is my husband coming?

MRS PAGE.   Ay, in good sadness,[7] is he; and talks of the basket too, howsoever he hath had intelligence.

MRS FORD.   We'll try that; for I'll appoint my men to carry the basket again, to meet him at the door with it, as they did last time.

MRS PAGE.   Nay, but he'll be here presently: let's go dress him like the witch of Brentford.

MRS FORD.   I'll first direct my men what they shall do with the basket. Go up; I'll bring linen for him straight.   [Exit.

MRS PAGE.   Hang him, dishonest varlet! we cannot misuse him enough.
We'll leave a proof, by that which we will do,
Wives may be merry, and yet honest too:
We do not act that often jest and laugh;
'Tis old, but true,—Still swine eats all the draff.   [Exit.

Re-enter MISTRESS FORD *with two* Servants

MRS FORD.   Go, sirs, take the basket again on your shoulders: your master is hard at door; if he bid you set it down, obey him: quickly, dispatch.   [Exit.

FIRST SERV.   Come, come, take it up.

SEC. SERV.   Pray heaven it be not full of knight again.

FIRST SERV.   I hope not; I had as lief bear so much lead.

Enter FORD, PAGE, SHALLOW, CAIUS, *and* SIR HUGH EVANS

FORD.   Ay, but if it prove true, Master Page, have you any way then to unfool me again? Set down the basket, villain! Somebody call my wife. Youth in a basket!—O you pandarly rascals! there's a knot, a ging, a pack,[8] a conspiracy against me: now shall the devil be shamed.—What, wife, I say!—Come, come forth! Behold what honest clothes you send forth to bleaching!

PAGE.   Why, this passes, Master Ford; you are not to go loose any longer; you must be pinioned.

---

[7]*in good sadness*] in sober earnest.
[8]*a knot, a ging, a pack*] an assembly, a gang, a crowd.

EVANS. Why, this is lunatics! this is mad as a mad dog!
SHAL. Indeed, Master Ford, this is not well, indeed.
FORD. So say I too, sir.

Re-enter MISTRESS FORD

Come hither, Mistress Ford; Mistress Ford, the honest woman,
the modest wife, the virtuous creature, that hath the jealous fool
to her husband! I suspect without cause, mistress, do I?
MRS FORD. Heaven be my witness you do, if you suspect me in any
dishonesty.
FORD. Well said, brazen-face! hold it out.[9] Come forth, sirrah!
[*Pulling clothes out of the basket.*
PAGE. This passes!
MRS FORD. Are you not ashamed? let the clothes alone.
FORD. I shall find you anon.
EVANS. 'T is unreasonable! Will you take up your wife's clothes?
Come away.
FORD. Empty the basket, I say!
MRS FORD. Why, man, why?
FORD. Master Page, as I am a man, there was one conveyed out of my
house yesterday in this basket: why may not he be there again? In
my house I am sure he is: my intelligence is true; my jealousy is
reasonable. Pluck me out all the linen.
MRS FORD. If you find a man there, he shall die a flea's death.
PAGE. Here's no man.
SHAL. By my fidelity, this is not well, Master Ford; this wrongs you.
EVANS. Master Ford, you must pray, and not follow the imaginations
of your own heart: this is jealousies.
FORD. Well, he's not here I seek for.
PAGE. No, nor nowhere else but in your brain.
FORD. Help to search my house this one time. If I find not what I
seek, show no colour for my extremity;[10] let me for ever be your
table-sport; let them say of me, "As jealous as Ford, that searched
a hollow walnut for his wife's leman." Satisfy me once more; once
more search with me.
MRS FORD. What, ho, Mistress Page! come you and the old woman
down; my husband will come into the chamber.
FORD. Old woman! what old woman's that?
MRS FORD. Why, it is my maid's aunt of Brentford.
FORD. A witch, a quean, an old cozening quean! Have I not forbid
her my house? She comes of errands, does she? We are simple

---

[9]*hold it out*] keep it up.
[10]*show no colour . . . extremity*] admit no reasonable pretext for my extreme courses.

men: we do not know what's brought to pass under the profession
of fortune-telling. She works by charms, by spells, by the figure,[11]
and such daubery[12] as this is, beyond our element: we know nothing. Come down, you witch, you hag, you; come down, I say!

MRS FORD.   Nay, good, sweet husband!—Good gentlemen, let him
not strike the old woman.

Re-enter FALSTAFF *in woman's clothes, and* MISTRESS PAGE

MRS PAGE.   Come, Mother Prat: come, give me your hand.
FORD.   I'll prat her. [*Beating him*] Out of my door, you witch, you
hag,[13] you baggage, you polecat, you ronyon! out, out! I'll conjure
you, I'll fortune-tell you.   [*Exit* FALSTAFF.
MRS PAGE.   Are you not ashamed? I think you have killed the poor
woman.
MRS FORD.   Nay, he will do it. 'T is a goodly credit for you.
FORD.   Hang her, witch!
EVANS.   By yea and no, I think the 'oman is a witch indeed: I like
not when a 'oman has a great peard; I spy a great peard under his
muffler.
FORD.   Will you follow, gentlemen? I beseech you, follow; see but the
issue of my jealousy: if I cry out thus upon no trial, never trust me
when I open again.[14]
PAGE.   Let's obey his humour a little further: come, gentlemen.
                    [*Exeunt* FORD, PAGE, SHAL., CAIUS, *and* EVANS.
MRS PAGE.   Trust me, he beat him most pitifully.
MRS FORD.   Nay, by the mass, that he did not; he beat him most un-
pitifully methought.
MRS PAGE.   I'll have the cudgel hallowed and hung o'er the altar; it
hath done meritorious service.
MRS FORD.   What think you? may we, with the warrant of woman-
hood and the witness of a good conscience, pursue him with any
further revenge?
MRS PAGE.   The spirit of wantonness is, sure, scared out of him: if the
devil have him not in fee-simple, with fine and recovery, he will
never, I think, in the way of waste, attempt us again.
MRS FORD.   Shall we tell our husbands how we have served him?

---

[11]*by the figure*] by casting the figure, by calculating the horoscope.
[12] *daubery*] cheating. The verb "daub" is similarly used.
[13]*hag*] This is the reading of the Third and later Folios. The First and Second Folios
read *rag*. But *hag* has already been used. "Rag" was, however, occasionally employed
as a term of contempt.
[14]*cry out . . . again*] The expression is drawn from hunting, in which the hounds cry out
when they find the scent. "Open" means "open mouth," "give tongue."

MRS PAGE.   Yes, by all means; if it be but to scrape the figures[15] out of your husband's brains. If they can find in their hearts the poor unvirtuous fat knight shall be any further afflicted, we two will still be the ministers.

MRS FORD.   I'll warrant they'll have him publicly shamed: and methinks there would be no period to the jest, should he not be publicly shamed.

MRS PAGE.   Come, to the forge with it, then; shape it: I would not have things cool.   [*Exeunt.*

SCENE III. *A Room in the Garter Inn.*

Enter HOST *and* BARDOLPH

BARD.   Sir, the Germans desire to have three of your horses: the duke himself will be to-morrow at court, and they are going to meet him.

HOST.   What duke should that be comes so secretly? I hear not of him in the court. Let me speak with the gentlemen: they speak English?

BARD.   Ay, sir; I'll call them to you.

HOST.   They shall have my horses; but I'll make them pay; I'll sauce them: they have had my house a week at command; I have turned away my other guests: they must come off; I'll sauce them. Come.
                                    [*Exeunt.*

SCENE IV. *A Room in Ford's House.*

Enter PAGE, FORD, MISTRESS PAGE, MISTRESS FORD, *and* SIR HUGH EVANS

EVANS.   'T is one of the best discretions of a 'oman as ever I did look upon.

PAGE.   And did he send you both these letters at an instant?

MRS PAGE.   With a quarter of an hour.

FORD.   Pardon me, wife. Henceforth do what thou wilt;
I rather will suspect the sun with cold
Than thee with wantonness: now doth thy honour stand,
In him that was of late an heretic,
As firm as faith.

---

[15]*figures*] imaginary forms, ideas.

PAGE.   'T is well, 't is well; no more:
   Be not as extreme in submission
   As in offence.
   But let our plot go forward: let our wives
   Yet once again, to make us public sport,
   Appoint a meeting with this old fat fellow,
   Where we may take him, and disgrace him for it.

FORD.   There is no better way than that they spoke of.

PAGE.   How? to send him word they'll meet him in the Park at midnight? Fie, fie! he'll never come.

EVANS.   You say he has been thrown in the rivers, and has been grievously peaten, as an old 'oman: methinks there should be terrors in
   him that he should not come; methinks his flesh is punished, he
   shall have no desires.

PAGE.   So think I too.

MRS FORD.   Devise but how you'll use him when he comes,
   And let us two devise to bring him thither.

MRS PAGE.   There is an old tale goes that Herne the hunter,
   Sometime a keeper here in Windsor forest,
   Doth all the winter-time, at still midnight,
   Walk round about an oak, with great ragg'd horns;
   And there he blasts the tree, and takes the cattle,[1]
   And makes milch-kine yield blood, and shakes a chain
   In a most hideous and dreadful manner:
   You have heard of such a spirit; and well you know
   The superstitious idle-headed eld
   Received, and did deliver to our age,
   This tale of Herne the hunter for a truth.

PAGE.   Why, yet there want not many that do fear
   In deep of night to walk by this Herne's oak:
   But what of this?

MRS FORD.   Marry, this is our device;
   That Falstaff at that oak shall meet with us.[2]

PAGE.   Well, let it not be doubted but he'll come:
   And in this shape when you have brought him thither,
   What shall be done with him? what is your plot?

MRS PAGE.   That likewise have we thought upon, and thus:
   Nan Page my daughter and my little son
   And three or four more of their growth we'll dress

---

[1] *takes the cattle*] strikes the cattle with disease.

[2] *Marry . . . us*] This speech is given far more explicitly in the First and early Quartos, and thence most editors derive a third line, *Disguis'd like Herne with huge horns on his head.* Some such insertion seems necessary to explain the next speech.

Like urchins, ouphes and fairies, green and white,
With rounds of waxen tapers on their heads,
And rattles in their hands: upon a sudden,
As Falstaff, she, and I, are newly met,
Let them from forth a sawpit rush at once
With some diffused song: upon their sight,
We two in great amazedness will fly:
Then let them all encircle him about,
And, fairy-like, to pinch[3] the unclean knight;
And ask him why, that hour of fairy revel,
In their so sacred paths he dares to tread
In shape profane.

MRS FORD.   And till he tell the truth,
Let the supposed fairies pinch him sound,
And burn him with their tapers.

MRS PAGE.   The truth being known,
We'll all present ourselves, dis-horn the spirit,
And mock him home to Windsor.

FORD.   The children must
Be practised well to this, or they'll ne'er do 't.

EVANS.   I will teach the children their behaviours; and I will be like a
jack-an-apes also, to burn the knight with my taber.

FORD.   That will be excellent. I'll go buy them vizards.

MRS PAGE.   My Nan shall be the queen of all the fairies,
Finely attired in a robe of white.

PAGE.   That silk will I go buy. [*Aside*] And in that time
Shall Master Slender steal my Nan away,
And marry her at Eton. Go send to Falstaff straight.

FORD.   Nay, I'll to him again in name of Brook:
He'll tell me all his purpose: sure, he'll come.

MRS PAGE.   Fear not you that. Go get us properties
And tricking for our fairies.

EVANS.   Let us about it: it is admirable pleasures and fery honest
knaveries.   [*Exeunt* PAGE, FORD, *and* EVANS.

MRS PAGE.   Go, Mistress Ford,
Send quickly to Sir John, to know his mind.   [*Exit* MRS FORD.
I'll to the doctor: he hath my good will,
And none but he, to marry with Nan Page.
That Slender, though well landed, is an idiot;
And he my husband best of all affects.

---

[3]*to pinch*] This is the Folio reading, for which editors have substituted *to-pinch*, where
"to" is regarded as an intensive prefix. Such a form is found elsewhere.

The doctor is well money'd, and his friends
Potent at court: he, none but he, shall have her,
Though twenty thousand worthier come to crave her.   [*Exit.*

SCENE V. *A Room in the Garter Inn.*

Enter HOST *and* SIMPLE

HOST. What wouldst thou have, boor? what, thickskin? speak, breathe, discuss; brief, short, quick, snap.

SIM. Marry, sir, I come to speak with Sir John Falstaff from Master Slender.

HOST. There's his chamber, his house, his castle, his standing-bed, and truckle-bed; 't is painted about with the story of the Prodigal, fresh and new. Go knock and call; he'll speak like an Anthropophaginian[1] unto thee: knock, I say.

SIM. There's an old woman, a fat woman, gone up into his chamber: I'll be so bold as stay, sir, till she come down; I come to speak with her, indeed.

HOST. Ha! a fat woman! the knight may be robbed: I'll call.—Bully knight! bully Sir John! speak from thy lungs military: art thou there? it is thine host, thine Ephesian,[2] calls.

FAL. [*Above*] How now, mine host!

HOST. Here's a Bohemian-Tartar[3] tarries the coming down of thy fat woman. Let her descend, bully, let her descend; my chambers are honourable: fie! privacy? fie!

Enter FALSTAFF

FAL. There was, mine host, an old fat woman even now with me; but she's gone.

SIM. Pray you, sir, was 't not the wise woman of Brentford?

FAL. Ay, marry, was it, muscle-shell:[4] what would you with her?

SIM. My master, sir, Master Slender, sent to her, seeing her go thorough the streets, to know, sir, whether one Nym, sir, that beguiled him of a chain, had the chain or no.

---

[1]*Anthropophaginian*] "Anthropophagi" was the accepted term for man-eaters or cannibals. "Anthropophaginian" is mine host's invention, and is coined on the analogy of "Carthaginian."
[2]*Ephesian*] This word has much the same significance in Elizabethan slang as "Corinthian," *i.e.*, a good fellow, a man of mettle.
[3]*Bohemian-Tartar*] a grandiloquent periphrasis for "gipsy."
[4]*muscle-shell*] Simple's lips are agape, like the shells of a mussel.

FAL. I spake with the old woman about it.

SIM. And what says she, I pray, sir?

FAL. Marry, she says that the very same man that beguiled Master Slender of his chain cozened him of it.

SIM. I would I could have spoken with the woman herself; I had other things to have spoken with her too from him.

FAL. What are they? let us know.

HOST. Ay, come; quick.

SIM. I may not conceal[5] them, sir.

HOST. Conceal them, or thou diest.

SIM. Why, sir, they were nothing but about Mistress Anne Page; to know if it were my master's fortune to have her or no.

FAL. 'T is, 't is his fortune.

SIM. What, sir?

FAL. To have her, or no. Go; say the woman told me so.

SIM. May I be bold to say so, sir?

FAL. Ay, sir; like who more bold.

SIM. I thank your worship: I shall make my master glad with these tidings. [*Exit.*

HOST. Thou art clerkly, thou art clerkly, Sir John. Was there a wise woman with thee?

FAL. Ay, that there was, mine host; one that hath taught me more wit than ever I learned before in my life; and I paid nothing for it neither, but was paid[6] for my learning.

Enter BARDOLPH

BARD. Out, alas, sir! cozenage, mere cozenage!

HOST. Where be my horses? speak well of them, varletto.

BARD. Run away with the cozeners: for so soon as I came beyond Eton, they threw me off, from behind one of them, in a slough of mire; and set spurs and away, like three German devils, three Doctor Faustuses.[7]

HOST. They are gone but to meet the duke, villain: do not say they be fled, Germans are honest men.

Enter SIR HUGH EVANS

EVANS. Where is mine host?

HOST. What is the matter, sir?

EVANS. Have a care of your entertainments: there is a friend of mine

---

[5]*conceal*] blunder for "reveal."

[6]*was paid*] was paid out, punished, beaten.

[7]*Faustuses*] a probable reference to Marlowe's tragedy of *Dr. Faustus.*

come to town, tells me there is three cozen-germans[8] that has cozened all the hosts of Readins, of Maidenhead, of Colebrook, of
horses and money. I tell you for good will, look you: you are wise,
and full of gibes and vlouting-stocks,[9] and 't is not convenient you
should be cozened. Fare you well. [*Exit.*

Enter DOCTOR CAIUS

CAIUS. Vere is mine host de Jarteer?
HOST. Here, master doctor, in perplexity and doubtful dilemma.
CAIUS. I cannot tell vat is dat: but it is tell-a me dat you make grand
preparation for a duke de Jamany: by my trot, dere is no duke dat
the court is known to come. I tell you for good vill: adieu. [*Exit.*
HOST. Hue and cry, villain, go!—Assist me, knight.—I am undone!—
Fly, run, hue and cry, villain!—I am undone!
[*Exeunt* HOST *and* BARD.
FAL. I would all the world might be cozened; for I have been cozened
and beaten too. If it should come to the ear of the court, how I
have been transformed, and how my transformation hath been
washed and cudgelled, they would melt me out of my fat drop by
drop, and liquor fishermen's boots with me: I warrant they would
whip me with their fine wits till I were as crest-fallen as a dried
pear. I never prospered since I forswore myself at primero. Well, if
my wind were but long enough to say my prayers, I would repent.

Enter MISTRESS QUICKLY

Now, whence come you?
QUICK. From the two parties, forsooth.
FAL. The devil take one party, and his dam the other! And so they
shall be both bestowed. I have suffered more for their sakes, more
than the villanous inconstancy of man's disposition is able to bear.
QUICK. And have not they suffered? Yes, I warrant; speciously[10] one
of them; Mistress Ford, good heart, is beaten black and blue, that
you cannot see a white spot about her.

---

[8]*there is three cozen-germans*] There is a plain reference here to a contemporary
episode of historic importance. The First Quarto reads, *there is three sorts of cosen garmombles.* "Garmombles" seems to be a burlesque rendering of the German name
"Mompelgard." In 1592 Frederick, Duke of Wirtemberg, who was well known in
England during his stay by his subordinate title of Count Mompelgard, was granted
official permission to requisition post-horses free of charge—a grant which offended
innkeepers. Count Mompelgard seems to have actually visited inns at Reading,
Maidenhead, and Colebrook, the places mentioned in the text.
[9]*vlouting-stocks*] flouts.
[10]*speciously*] blunder for "especially."

FAL.   What tell'st thou me of black and blue? I was beaten myself into
all the colours of the rainbow; and I was like to be apprehended
for the witch of Brentford: but that my admirable dexterity of wit,
my counterfeiting the action of an old woman, delivered me, the
knave constable had set me i' the stocks, i' the common stocks, for
a witch.

QUICK.   Sir, let me speak with you in your chamber: you shall hear
how things go; and, I warrant, to your content. Here is a letter will
say somewhat. Good hearts, what ado here is to bring you together! Sure, one of you does not serve heaven well, that you are
so crossed.

FAL.   Come up into my chamber.   [*Exeunt.*

SCENE VI. *The Same. Another Room in the Garter Inn.*

Enter FENTON *and* HOST

HOST.   Master Fenton, talk not to me; my mind is heavy: I will give
over all.

FENT.   Yet hear me speak. Assist me in my purpose,
And, as I am a gentleman, I'll give thee
A hundred pound in gold more than your loss.

HOST.   I will hear you, Master Fenton; and I will at the least keep your
counsel.

FENT.   From time to time I have acquainted you
With the dear love I bear to fair Anne Page;
Who mutually hath answer'd my affection,
So far forth as herself might be her chooser,
Even to my wish: I have a letter from her
Of such contents as you will wonder at;
The mirth whereof so larded with my matter,
That neither singly can be manifested,
Without the show of both; fat Falstaff[1]
Hath a great scene: the image of the jest
I'll show you here at large. Hark, good mine host.
To-night at Herne's oak, just 'twixt twelve and one,
Must my sweet Nan present the Fairy Queen;
The purpose why, is here: in which disguise,
While other jests are something rank on foot,
Her father hath commanded her to slip

[1]*fat Falstaff*] The earlier Quartos insert *wherein* before *fat Falstaff*. The insertion seems
necessary to complete the line.

Away with Slender, and with him at Eton
Immediately to marry: she hath consented:
Now, sir,
Her mother, even strong against that match,
And firm for Doctor Caius, hath appointed
That he shall likewise shuffle her away,
While other sports are tasking of their minds,
And at the deanery, where a priest attends,
Straight marry her: to this her mother's plot
She seemingly obedient likewise hath
Made promise to the doctor. Now, thus it rests:
Her father means she shall be all in white;
And in that habit, when Slender sees his time
To take her by the hand and bid her go,
She shall go with him: her mother hath intended,
The better to denote her to the doctor,—
For they must all be mask'd and vizarded,—
That quaint in green she shall be loose enrobed,
With ribands pendent, flaring 'bout her head;
And when the doctor spies his vantage ripe,
To pinch her by the hand, and, on that token,
The maid hath given consent to go with him.

HOST.   Which means she to deceive, father or mother?

FENT.   Both, my good host, to go along with me:
And here it rests,—that you'll procure the vicar
To stay for me at church 'twixt twelve and one,
And, in the lawful name of marrying,
To give our hearts united ceremony.[2]

HOST.   Well, husband your device; I'll to the vicar:
Bring you the maid, you shall not lack a priest.

FENT.   So shall I evermore be bound to thee;
Besides, I'll make a present recompence.   [*Exeunt.*

---

[2]*united ceremony*] uniting ceremony, ceremony of union.

ACT V.

SCENE I. A Room in the Garter Inn.

Enter FALSTAFF *and* MISTRESS QUICKLY

FALSTAFF. Prithee, no more prattling; go. I'll hold. This is the third
time; I hope good luck lies in odd numbers. Away! go. They say
there is divinity in odd numbers, either in nativity, chance, or
death. Away!

QUICK. I'll provide you a chain; and I'll do what I can to get you a
pair of horns.

FAL. Away, I say; time wears: hold up your head, and mince.[1]

[Exit MRS QUICKLY.

Enter FORD

How now, Master Brook! Master Brook, the matter will be known
to-night, or never. Be you in the Park about midnight, at Herne's
oak, and you shall see wonders.

FORD. Went you not to her yesterday, sir, as you told me you had
appointed?

FAL. I went to her, Master Brook, as you see, like a poor old man: but
I came from her, Master Brook, like a poor old woman. That same
knave Ford, her husband, hath the finest mad devil of jealousy in
him, Master Brook, that ever governed frenzy. I will tell you:—he
beat me grievously, in the shape of a woman; for in the shape of
man, Master Brook, I fear not Goliath with a weaver's beam; because I know also life is a shuttle.[2] I am in haste; go along with me:
I'll tell you all, Master Brook. Since I plucked geese,[3] played tru-
ant, and whipped top, I knew not what 't was to be beaten till
lately. Follow me: I'll tell you strange things of this knave Ford, on

[1]*mince*] walk with affected gait, with short steps.
[2]*life is a shuttle*] Cf. *Job*, vii, 6: "My days are swifter than a weaver's *shuttle.*"
[3]*plucked geese*] stripped living geese of their feathers as boys were wont to do.

64

whom to-night I will be revenged, and I will deliver his wife into
your hand. Follow. Strange things in hand, Master Brook! Follow.
                                                        [*Exeunt.*

SCENE II. *Windsor Park.*

Enter PAGE, SHALLOW, *and* SLENDER

PAGE.   Come, come; we'll couch i' the castle-ditch till we see the light
of our fairies. Remember, son Slender, my daughter.

SLEN.   Ay, forsooth; I have spoke with her, and we have a nay-word
how to know one another: I come to her in white, and cry, "mum;"
she cries "budget;"[1] and by that we know one another.

SHAL.   That's good too: but what needs either your "mum" or her
"budget"? the white will decipher her well enough. It hath struck
ten o'clock.

PAGE.   The night is dark; light and spirits will become it well. Heaven
prosper our sport! No man means evil but the devil, and we shall
know him by his horns. Let's away; follow me.   [*Exeunt.*

SCENE III. *A Street Leading to the Park.*

Enter MISTRESS PAGE, MISTRESS FORD, *and* DOCTOR CAIUS

MRS PAGE.   Master Doctor, my daughter is in green: when you see
your time, take her by the hand, away with her to the deanery, and
dispatch it quickly. Go before into the Park: we two must go together.

CAIUS.   I know vat I have to do. Adieu.

MRS PAGE.   Fare you well, sir. [*Exit* CAIUS.] My husband will not re-
joice so much at the abuse of Falstaff as he will chafe at the doctor's marrying my daughter: but 't is no matter; better a little chid-
ing than a great deal of heart-break.

MRS FORD.   Where is Nan now and her troop of fairies, and the Welsh
devil Hugh?

MRS PAGE.   They are all couched in a pit hard by Herne's oak, with
obscured lights; which, at the very instant of Falstaff's and our
meeting, they will at once display to the night.

MRS FORD.   That cannot choose but amaze him.

---

[1]*"mum"* . . . *"budget"*] Both were whispered exclamations implying the need of keeping secrets.

MRS PAGE.   If he be not amazed, he will be mocked; if he be amazed, he will every way be mocked.
MRS FORD.   We'll betray him finely.
MRS PAGE.   Against such lewdsters and their lechery
Those that betray them do no treachery.
MRS FORD.   The hour draws on. To the oak, to the oak!   [*Exeunt.*

SCENE IV. *Windsor Park.*

Enter SIR HUGH EVANS *disguised, with others as Fairies*

EVANS.   Trib, trib, fairies; come; and remember your parts: be pold, I pray you; follow me into the pit; and when I give the watch-'ords, do as I pid you: come, come; trib, trib.   [*Exeunt.*

SCENE V. *Another Part of the Park.*

Enter FALSTAFF *disguised as Herne*

FAL.   The Windsor bell hath struck twelve; the minute draws on. Now, the hot-blooded gods assist me! Remember, Jove, thou wast a bull for thy Europa; love set on thy horns. O powerful love! that, in some respects, makes a beast a man; in some other, a man a beast. You were also, Jupiter, a swan for the love of Leda. O omnipotent Love! how near the god drew to the complexion of a goose! A fault done first in the form of a beast;—O Jove, a beastly fault! And then another fault in the semblance of a fowl;—think on 't, Jove; a foul fault! When gods have hot backs, what shall poor men do? For me, I am here a Windsor stag; and the fattest, I think, i' the forest. Send me a cool rut-time, Jove, or who can blame me to piss my tallow?—Who comes here? my doe?

Enter MISTRESS FORD *and* MISTRESS PAGE

MRS FORD.   Sir John! art thou there, my deer? my male deer?
FAL.   My doe with the black scut! Let the sky rain potatoes; let it thunder to the tune of Green Sleeves, hail kissing-comfits,[1] and snow eringoes;[2] let there come a tempest of provocation, I will shelter me here.

[1]*kissing-comfits*] perfumed sugar plums, which made the breath sweet.
[2]*rain potatoes*] Potatoes and "eringoes" (the candied root of the sea holly) were in early days reckoned aphrodisiacs. Potatoes and eringoes are frequently mentioned together by Elizabethan dramatists in the same significance as in the text.

MRS FORD.   Mistress Page is come with me, sweetheart.

FAL.   Divide me like a bribe buck,[3] each a haunch: I will keep my
sides to myself, my shoulders for the fellow of this walk,[4] and my
horns I bequeath your husbands. Am I a woodman, ha? Speak I
like Herne the hunter? Why, now is Cupid a child of conscience;
he makes restitution. As I am a true spirit, welcome!

                                                        [*Noise within.*

MRS PAGE.   Alas, what noise?

MRS FORD.   Heaven forgive our sins!

FAL.   What should this be?

MRS FORD. ⎫
                 ⎬ Away, away!   [*They run off.*
MRS PAGE. ⎭

FAL.   I think the devil will not have me damned, lest the oil that's in
me should set hell on fire; he would never else cross me thus.

Enter SIR HUGH EVANS, *disguised as before;* PISTOL, *as Hobgoblin;*
  MISTRESS QUICKLY, ANNE PAGE, *and others, as Fairies, with
  tapers.*[5]

QUICK.   Fairies, black, grey, green, and white,
You moonshine revellers, and shades of night,
You orphan heirs of fixed destiny,[6]
Attend your office and your quality.
Crier Hobgoblin, make the fairy oyes.

PIST.   Elves, list your names; silence, you airy toys.
Cricket, to Windsor chimneys shalt thou leap:
Where fires thou find'st unraked and hearths unswept,
There pinch the maids as blue as bilberry:
Our radiant queen hates sluts and sluttery.

FAL.   They are fairies; he that speaks to them shall die:
I'll wink and couch: no man their works must eye.

                                              [*Lies down upon his face.*

EVANS.   Where's Bede?[7] Go you, and where you find a maid
That, ere she sleep, has thrice her prayers said,
Raise up the organs of her fantasy;
Sleep she as sound as careless infancy:

---

[3]*bribe buck*] Theobald's emendation of the early reading, *brib'd buck.* It probably means
a buck of the fine quality bred for giving away as bribes or presents.

[4]*the fellow of this walk*] the forester or gamekeeper.

[5]*Enter . . . tapers*] In the early Quartos this stage direction reads thus: "Enter Sir Hugh
like a Satyre, and boyes drest like Fayries, Mistresse Quickly, like the queene of
Fayries; they sing a song about him and afterward speake."

[6]*orphan heirs . . . destiny*] miraculously conceived inheritors of immortality.

[7]*Bede*] This is the name given to the fairy messenger in the Folios. The early Quartos
read *Pead,* which is probably more in keeping with Sir Hugh's ordinary dialect.

But those as sleep and think not on their sins,
Pinch them, arms, legs, backs, shoulders, sides, and shins.

QUICK.　About, about;
Search Windsor Castle, elves, within and out:
Strew good luck, ouphes, on every sacred room;
That it may stand till the perpetual doom,
In state as wholesome as in state 't is fit,
Worthy the owner, and the owner it.
The several chairs of order look you scour
With juice of balm and every precious flower:
Each fair instalment[8] coat, and several crest,
With loyal blazon, evermore be blest!
And nightly, meadow-fairies, look you sing,
Like to the Garter's compass, in a ring:
Th' expressure that it bears, green let it be,
More fertile-fresh than all the field to see;
And *Honi soit qui mal y pense* write
In emerald tufts, flowers purple, blue, and white;
Like sapphire, pearl, and rich embroidery,
Buckled below fair knighthood's bending knee:
Fairies use flowers for their charactery.[9]
Away; disperse: but till 't is one o'clock,
Our dance of custom round about the oak
Of Herne the hunter, let us not forget.

EVANS.　Pray you, lock hand in hand; yourselves in order set;
And twenty glow-worms shall our lanterns be,
To guide our measure round about the tree
But, stay; I smell a man of middle-earth.[10]

FAL.　Heavens defend me from that Welsh fairy, lest he transform me
to a piece of cheese!

PIST.　Vile worm, thou wast o'erlook'd even in thy birth.

QUICK.　With trial-fire touch me his finger-end:
If he be chaste, the flame will back descend,
And turn him[11] to no pain; but if he start,
It is the flesh of a corrupted heart.

PIST.　A trial, come.

EVANS.　　　　　　　Come, will this wood take fire?
　　　　　　　　　　　　　　　[They burn him with their tapers.

---

[8]*instalment*] The word which commonly means "installation" seems to signify here the "stall" of a knight of the Garter.

[9]*charactery*] written cipher; often used in the sense of "shorthand."

[10]*middle*] a conventional poetic epithet. In the current astronomical system the earth was the *middle* region of the universe, of which the upper region was the home of God and the lower region the abode of the fairies.

[11]*turn him*] put him, a common contemporary usage.

FAL.   Oh, Oh, Oh!
QUICK.   Corrupt, corrupt, and tainted in desire!
    About him, fairies; sing a scornful rhyme;
    And, as you trip, still pinch him to your time.

SONG

        Fie on sinful fantasy![12]
        Fie on lust and luxury![13]
        Lust is but a bloody fire,[14]
        Kindled with unchaste desire,
        Fed in heart, whose flames aspire,
        As thoughts do blow them, higher and higher.
            Pinch him, fairies, mutually;
            Pinch him for his villany;
        Pinch him, and burn him, and turn him about,
        Till candles and starlight and moonshine be out.

During this song they pinch FALSTAFF. DOCTOR CAIUS *comes one way,*
    and steals away a boy in green; SLENDER *another way, and takes*
    off a boy in white; and FENTON *comes, and steals away* MRS
    ANNE PAGE. *A noise of hunting is heard within. All the Fairies run*
    away. FALSTAFF *pulls off his buck's head, and rises.*[15]

Enter PAGE, FORD, MISTRESS PAGE *and* MISTRESS FORD

PAGE.   Nay, do not fly; I think we have watch'd you now:
    Will none but Herne the hunter serve your turn?
MRS PAGE.   I pray you, come, hold up the jest no higher.
    Now, good Sir John, how like you Windsor wives?
    See you these, husband? do not these fair yokes[16]
    Become the forest better than the town?
FORD.   Now, sir, who's a cuckold now? Master Brook, Falstaff's
    a knave, a cuckoldly knave; here are his horns, Master Brook:
    and, Master Brook, he hath enjoyed nothing of Ford's but his buck-
    basket, his cudgel, and twenty pounds of money, which must be
    paid to Master Brook; his horses are arrested for it, Master Brook.

---

[12]*fantasy*] love.
[13]*luxury*] lasciviousness, incontinence.
[14]*bloody fire*] fire of blood.
[15]*During this song . . . rises*] This stage direction is absent from the First Folio, but it fig-
    ures in the early Quartos, whence Theobald and succeeding editors have borrowed it.
[16]*fair yokes*] This is the reading of the First Folio, which the Second and later Folios
    changed to *okes, i.e.* oaks. The reference, of course, is to the horns, which sometimes
    take a shape resembling yokes for cattle. It is less reasonable to identify the horns with
    the branches of an oak tree.

MRS FORD.   Sir John, we have had ill luck; we could never meet. I
will never take you for my love again; but I will always count you
my deer.

FAL.   I do begin to perceive that I am made an ass.

FORD.   Ay, and an ox too: both the proofs are extant.

FAL.   And these are not fairies? I was three or four times in the thought
they were not fairies: and yet the guiltiness of my mind, the sudden surprise of my powers, drove the grossness of the foppery into
a received belief, in despite of the teeth of[17] all rhyme and reason,
that they were fairies. See now how wit may be made a Jack-a-
Lent, when 't is upon ill employment!

EVANS.   Sir John Falstaff, serve Got, and leave your desires, and fairies
will not pinse you.

FORD.   Well said, fairy Hugh.

EVANS.   And leave you your jealousies too, I pray you.

FORD.   I will never mistrust my wife again, till thou art able to woo her
in good English.

FAL.   Have I laid my brain in the sun and dried it, that it wants matter
to prevent so gross o'erreaching as this? Am I ridden with a Welsh
goat too? shall I have a coxcomb of frize?[18] 'T is time I were
choked with a piece of toasted cheese.

EVANS.   Seese is not good to give putter; your pelly is all putter.

FAL.   "Seese" and "putter"? Have I lived to stand at the taunt of one
that makes fritters of English? This is enough to be the decay of
lust and late-walking through the realm.

MRS PAGE.   Why, Sir John, do you think, though we would have
thrust virtue out of our hearts by the head and shoulders, and have
given ourselves without scruple to hell, that ever the devil could
have made you our delight?

FORD.   What, a hodge-pudding? a bag of flax?

MRS PAGE.   A puffed man?

PAGE.   Old, cold, withered, and of intolerable entrails?

FORD.   And one that is as slanderous as Satan?

PAGE.   And as poor as Job?

FORD.   And as wicked as his wife?

EVANS.   And given to fornications, and to taverns, and sack, and wine,
and metheglins, and to drinkings, and swearings, and starings,
pribbles and prabbles?

FAL.   Well, I am your theme: you have the start of me; I am dejected;

---

[17]*despite of the teeth of*] An emphatic conjunction of "despite" and "in the teeth of."
[18]*a coxcomb of frize*] A professional fool's cap made of the rough woollen cloth which
was a leading Welsh manufacture.

I am not able to answer the Welsh flannel: ignorance itself is a plummet o'er me:[19] use me as you will.

FORD.   Marry, sir, we'll bring you to Windsor, to one Master Brook, that you have cozened of money, to whom you should have been a pandar: over and above that you have suffered, I think to repay that money will be a biting affliction.

PAGE.   Yet be cheerful, knight: thou shalt eat a posset to-night at my house; where I will desire thee to laugh at my wife, that now laughs at thee: tell her Master Slender hath married her daughter.

MRS PAGE. [*Aside*]   Doctors doubt that: if Anne Page be my daughter, she is, by this, Doctor Caius' wife.

Enter SLENDER

SLEN.   Whoa, ho! ho, father Page!

PAGE.   Son, how now! how now, son! have you dispatched?

SLEN.   Dispatched! I'll make the best in Gloucestershire know on 't; would I were hanged, la, else!

PAGE.   Of what, son?

SLEN.   I came yonder at Eton to marry Mistress Anne Page, and she's a great lubberly boy. If it had not been i' the church, I would have swinged him, or he should have swinged me. If I did not think it had been Anne Page, would I might never stir!—and 't is a post-master's boy.

PAGE.   Upon my life, then, you took the wrong.

SLEN.   What need you tell me that? I think so, when I took a boy for a girl. If I had been married to him, for all he was in woman's apparel, I would not have had him.

PAGE.   Why, this is your own folly. Did not I tell you how you should know my daughter by her garments?

SLEN.   I went to her in white, and cried "mum," and she cried "budget," as Anne and I had appointed; and yet it was not Anne, but a postmaster's boy.

MRS PAGE.   Good George, be not angry: I knew of your purpose; turned my daughter into green; and, indeed, she is now with the doctor at the deanery, and there married.

Enter CAIUS

CAIUS.   Vere is Mistress Page? By gar, I am cozened: I ha' married un garçon, a boy; un paysan, by gar, a boy; it is not Anne Page: by gar, I am cozened.

MRS PAGE.   Why, did you take her in green?

---

[19]*ignorance . . . plummet o'er me*] ignorance, helplessness overcomes me with its leaden weight. "Plummet" is the weight of lead attached to the "plumbline."

CAIUS.   Ay, by gar, and 't is a boy: by gar, I'll raise all Windsor.

[*Exit.*

FORD.   This is strange. Who hath got the right Anne?
PAGE.   My heart misgives me:—here comes Master Fenton.

Enter FENTON *and* ANNE PAGE

  How now, Master Fenton!
ANNE.   Pardon, good father! good my mother, pardon!
PAGE.   Now, mistress, how chance you went not with Master Slender?
MRS PAGE.   Why went you not with master doctor, maid?
FENT.   You do amaze her: hear the truth of it.
  You would have married her most shamefully,
  Where there was no proportion held in love.
  The truth is, she and I, long since contracted,
  Are now so sure that nothing can dissolve us.
  The offence is holy that she hath committed;
  And this deceit loses the name of craft,
  Of disobedience, or unduteous title;
  Since therein she doth evitate and shun
  A thousand irreligious cursed hours,
  Which forced marriage would have brought upon her.
FORD.   Stand not amazed; here is no remedy:
  In love the heavens themselves do guide the state;
  Money buys lands, and wives are sold by fate.
FAL.   I am glad, though you have ta'en a special stand[20] to strike at me,
  that your arrow hath glanced.
PAGE.   Well, what remedy? Fenton, heaven give thee joy!
  What cannot be eschew'd must be embraced.
FAL.   When night-dogs run, all sorts of deer are chased.
MRS PAGE.   Well, I will muse no further. Master Fenton,
  Heaven give you many, many merry days!
  Good husband, let us every one go home,
  And laugh this sport o'er by a country fire;
  Sir John and all.
FORD.   Let it be so. Sir John,
  To Master Brook you yet shall hold your word;
  For he to-night shall lie with Mistress Ford.

[*Exeunt.*

---

[20]*stand*] a hiding place in the forest, whence the huntsman aims his arrow at the deer.